To my parents, with love

*Material for tractor drawings kindly
lent by Mr Cecil Wray of Killylea,
All-Ireland Ploughing Champion*

Contents

	Illustrations	xi
	Foreword	xv

Part One | **Ireland: July 1941 – April 1943** | **1**
Chapter One | Wartime Holiday | 3
Chapter Two | First Post in Ballymena | 7
Chapter Three | 'Short Intermission' | 19
Chapter Four | Postal Censorship, Belfast | 23
Chapter Five | Life Class, Cycling, The Flat | 31
Chapter Six | Cycling Tour in the West | 37
Chapter Seven | Friends and Decisions | 55

Part Two | **England: Women's Land Army
May 1943 – October 1945** | **63**
Chapter One | The Women's Land Army, Warwickshire | 65
Chapter Two | Ashow Hostel, Near Kenilworth | 81
Chapter Three | Tractor Depot, Leamington Spa | 85
Chapter Four | Stoneleigh Abbey | 97
Chapter Five | Thrashing | 105
Chapter Six | At Mrs Wilkinson's | 115
Chapter Seven | Haymaking and Harvest | 125
Chapter Eight | Lowland Farm, Oxhill | 141
Chapter Nine | Hill Farm, Shipston on Stour | 153

Illustrations

Map   *Frontispiece*

Haycocks, Carrigart and the north Donegal mountains   2

Going for turf near Downings, on the Atlantic Drive   2

The 'evacuee' aunt at Miss Wilson's   7

Miss Elsie Patton, head of English, Ballymera   8

Kennedy   14

The Square, Warrenpoint on a fair day   21

Postal Censorship   23

Laura at the Mill-dam near Warrenpoint   26

Lurigedan, Co. Antrim   29

It's a long way to Ballynahinch   32

Laura Sketching   39

Thatcher near Rossnowlagh, Co. Donegal   39

Glencolumbkille – next land America   41

Laura in the hotel at Malinmore   43

In a cottage near Ardara   45

Lough Gill, Co. Sligo   49

The Devany Family, Easky, Co. Sligo   50

Cottage in Co. Leitrim   50

Ben Bulben, north of Sligo Bay   52

Honor, Maeve, Mary, Jill, Rosa and Laura reading cups in
the flat, 83 Malone Avenue, Belfast   55

Peaceful Wartime

Jill at Warrenpoint   61

Jill on Rostrevor Mountain   61

Betty, Ellis, Joan, Nelly and Margaret at Idlicote Manor   64

Percy and Pony   67

Half of Idlicote village.   67

Betty, Iris, Jill and Roland weeding potatoes   69

Elevator   69

Roland, our field work instructor, Idlicote   71

Haymaking at Idlicote Manor farm   73

Eddie and Alice   74

What it looks like in the advertisements   77

Censored envelope   79

Laurie and Fred   86

Laurie and the Italians ricking beans   88

Ellis and Fordson at Three Gates   91

Joan, Margaret, Ferruccio and Ernie carrying wheat   93

Dinner-time; Margaret, the cook and his mate   93

'Giocoso'   95

Stoneleigh Abbey   98

Stoneleigh Abbey Gatehouse   103

Clearing-up   106

Thrashing-gang lunch   106

Ben   108

Bashing up lime to spread   109

'Tripping' the plough   110

Mrs Wilkinson with Robert and Chris, aged four and one   116

Water supply round in the wood (pump for 4 cottages)   119

The Kennels, four cottages   119

George, Phyl and Ben unloading manure   126

Illustrations

Phyl and Ellis wiring, Fred on the baler 127

Ben, Phyl, Mario ald Mary 128

George and Mary, loading sheaves 130

Fred Healey and Bunny cutting wheat 130

Ellis shucking wheat 133

Mrs Shire and Ann 142

Percy's morning drink 143

Hill Farm, Shipston-on-Stour 153

Mrs Watson and Graham 154

Graham milking with Alfa-Laval machines 156

Graham with part of the pedigree Ayrshire herd 157

Warrenpoint and Carlingford Lough 163

A Car Again! My parents in the nearly-new
Morgan 4-4, in 1945 163

Foreword

This fascinating, autobiographical account provides the reader with a rare insight into a key period of our history – namely the war years – stretching back almost six decades to the 1940s.

What makes it so interesting is that the narrative focuses mainly on the ordinary, everyday events and lives of people in both Ireland (North and South) and England during the era of conflict, 1941–45.

Ellis reminds us that, more than any war in the twentieth century, the Second World War was a **People's War** – in that the British Government of 1939–45 mobilised its populace and controlled its economy in a way that would be considered draconian today.

With some 1.5 million in the armed forces by spring of 1940 (the majority of them men) industrial production could only be expanded by the large-scale recruitment of women. From 1941 onwards conscription, which did not apply to Northern Ireland, was extended to single women, who could choose either to join one of the branches of the women's forces, work in a factory or become one of the **Land Girls** who were sent to help the farmers.

The writer gives us a most readable and uniquely detailed account of the agricultural work which took place in England – involving the Women's Land Army – assisted by Italian and German prisoners of war.

The text is accompanied by some enchanting photographs and line-drawings of work in the fields at harvest time and captures the sheer energy which was expended by farm labourers during this era. One can't help pondering how many of the present generation would countenance rising at 6.30 a.m. to labour in the fields from 8 a.m. to 5 p.m. – with a 3.30 p.m. finish on a Saturday!

Peaceful Wartime

Those survivors of the war years living in Ireland will be able to relate to the references in the text to Rationing, Blackout regulations and Postal Censorship.

Eire's neutrality of course, meant that a thriving cross-border trade in smuggling (particularly of foodstuffs) developed, and servicemen based in Northern Ireland found the Irish Republic a welcome retreat from a province faced with the rigours of wartime shortages.

Teachers and ex-teachers will be particularly intrigued by the revealing insight into classroom dynamics as they occurred in the 1940s – with the writer's account of her first teaching post in Ballymena.

I am delighted to have the opportunity to commend this enjoyable, interesting and educational book to the reader. I am particularly proud of the fact that the writer is a former mature student whom I had the pleasure of teaching some years back in a Sociology class in Armagh.

Intriguing and entertaining, the book records in a unique way civilian life in wartime. Older readers will be able to relate particularly closely to the events recorded in the text – even though for some the memories recalled may undoubtedly be painful. We should never forget the human cost – in terms of loss, suffering and sacrifice which war brings. For those too young to have lived in the 1940s the book will provide an invaluable understanding and appreciation of what life was like – as told by one who did actually experience and live through that memorable era.

Des McCready
(Further Education Lecturer)

Part One

Ireland: July 1941 – April 1943

Going for turf near Downings, on the Atlantic Drive.

Haycocks, Carrigart and the north Donegal mountains, from Muckish on the right to Errigal.

2

Chapter One

Wartime Holiday

ARLY IN JULY 1941, when I had finished my post-graduate year's teacher training in Trinity, my father and I set off for a tour of Donegal which we knew less well than other parts of the west coast. We stayed two nights in Bundoran, where the hotel had very good food and hideous yellowish paint in the corridors. Notices inside the gate warned us 'Beware of the golf balls' but as there were few playing, the threat was not severe. The town was peace - fully empty and nearly a third of the houses were thatched – in fact I hadn't seen so much thatch for years. We bathed on the strand, but the beach attendant kept blowing a whistle at us and afterwards told us, 'There's no swimmin' allowed'. In any case the waves didn't allow us in over our knees and when each wave had broken it carried me swiftly shorewards, sitting down, in nine inches of water.

We went along the south coast to Inver, where we were the only people staying. We spent two days in the Drumbeg Hotel and enjoyed a memorable high tea of delicious salmon-trout and salad. There was a lovely big walled garden with fruit trees all over the walls. Next day it poured rain till evening, when we went for a stroll through tall trees down towards the sea; it was so warm and damp that it felt quite tropical and enervating.

Next day we drove along the beautiful coast road by Killybegs and Carrick to Glencolumbkille in the far west, where the roads were hardly more than tracks. From there we went inland over the steep pass of Glengesh and down the corkscrew bends to Ardara, and made our way northwards past many lakes all full of white water-lilies, to Gweedore. The hotel, for quite a large one, had its funny ways. When

I asked for more gravy, the waiter brought it on a spare plate and solemnly poured it on to mine.

In the morning we went on up to the north-west corner of the county and round the Bloody Foreland by a fairly precipitous road through wild grand mountains. This marvellous district is headed by Errigal with its bold curving spine and conical peak. We gave a lift to a woman with a small boy and she was great crack; she had an accent strange to me that sounded like a mixture of Cork and Scots, and said, 'We get a wheen o' potatoes from Derry, and this year they were as dhry as if they were dug in August.' She lamented over the war: 'Sure there's no pleasure left for anybody, no American and English tourists that used to have whole meals laid out in a field, tablecloth and all, and give the children sweets and cake, and the people lifts in their cars.'

There was great digging of turf all over the country; some of the men here are earning a pound a day working from five in the morning till ten at night, an old man told us, but there was a slight strike on that morning for more pay. All the turf was for Dublin, because of the lack of coal from England. Our only native fuel had become tremendously important and was most ingeniously used to run pretty well everything that had formerly used coal; there were hilarious stories of trains refuelling from turf-ricks beside the track. Gas became a precious essence, turned on for only a few hours a day, but as it could not be completely turned off, there was 'the glimmer' which people in the towns used, to boil an illicit kettle very slowly.

It was a lovely light day. We went on to Carrigart, looked at the two shops displaying handwoven tweeds, and put up at a very nice hotel, Mrs Maguire's. I drove on our long trip through fine mountain country on fiercely twisty, hilly roads, at first with a very loose surface; we saw the Derryveagh mountains, then Glenveagh with its lough, and Lough Finn, which reminded me of Rob Roy's country.

The next day we went round the beautiful wild Rosguill Peninsula, the Atlantic Drive. In the afternoon we had to go to Derry to get petrol and then made our way up to Buncrana where we stayed the night at a little hotel called after Lough Swilly, 'The Lake of Shadows'. That evening we walked up the river, watched the fish jumping and

4

saw the men catching salmon in nets. We looked over Lough Swilly and the long range of hills on the far side with the sun setting behind them – not to mention the alcohol factory on the pier.

On our last day in the county, we drove up to Malin Head, the most northerly point of Ireland, for the last few miles along an appalling track. There were fine rocks and cliffs, with Irish Army soldiers on guard there perpetually. We came down the east side of the Inishowen peninsula through Moville to Derry, and had a very good run along the coast, with a night at Portstewart on the way home to Warrenpoint.

Chapter Two

First Post in Ballymena

I N SEPTEMBER, scanning the Belfast papers as usual for advertisements for teachers, I saw an urgent notice for two teachers wanted
in a Ballymena school 'to take between them the following subjects' ...
among them, English and French. I rang up next morning and went
over for interview in the afternoon. I wasn't very nervous; it was
really quite pleasant and the headmaster did most of the talking. I
told him I hadn't taught such big classes or any mixed ones in my
practice teaching in Dublin. He liked my qualifications, said it was
a temporary post, and after a week, wired to offer me the post. I felt
very unprepared, almost as if I hoped I wouldn't get the job, but had
to get a move on. As the following letter said to come immediately,
I did, but found I wasn't
needed till the next Monday.
My father and I searched the
place for lodgings, and found
some with a nice Miss Wilson,
and a restaurant where I could
have my lunch every week-day.

On Monday, 22nd of Sep-
tember, well after the
beginning of term, the head
took me round all my classes,
and I had to start finding out
at what stage they all were –
what a business! I had hoped
to do all that the week before.
There were 570 pupils, twenty-

The "evacuee" aunt at Miss Wilson's

five to thirty in a class, and a staff of twenty-five in the school, which combed a good part of County Antrim. I had about 130 names and the owners and their work to get to know, from 'Prep', aged from nine to ten, through B1, mostly brattish, and B2, up to C6, who had been pushed too fast in French into making little but mistakes; they had a lot to do in English, too, before they would be fit to take Junior Certificate next year. Most of these youngsters badly needed their certificates, junior and then senior, in order to get a job in a linen firm's office or something similar. The school was terribly exam-ridden and the children anxious.

My letter home says: 'The staff are very decent. Miss Patton, Trinity, is a dear; she is middle-aged, almost, with rather vague hair, an amusingly precise Northernish voice and a delightful expression.

Miss Elsie Patton, head of English, Ballymera.

She has a very droll way of describing her senior pupils and their doings.' With the other Trinity graduate, Ann, we were chatting about College, and Miss Patton told us the latest about Bobby Tate (Sir Robert, my erstwhile tutor) who has been taking all kinds of diplomas in dancing and is reported to have had two tables pushed together in some hotel, on which he executed a tap-dance. Miss Gibson has asked me to tea on Friday with another new teacher.'

My digs were pleasant enough, but I shared the sitting-room, in a clicking of knitting-needles, not only with Miss Wilson but with a family of friends of hers who were 'evacuated' from Belfast: father, mother, aunt and daughter who, with incredible patience, knitted whole jumpers in the learner style, taking her right hand off the needle and winding the wool round with it, saying 'I'm dead slow'. Her ambition, in spite of a slight lisp, was to be an elocution teacher, so she went to Belfast once a week for her lesson and worked for her diploma. She was afflicted by a perfect disease of politeness, and would hand you something, saying 'thank you'; I couldn't keep up with it.

'She was not strong when she was small; her mother calls her a 'home bird'. She apologises earnestly to the Almighty for my sins, over everything I eat.' I had to be flippant to my diary, but felt rather guilty because they were all very kind to me.

On Sundays after church and lunch they sat round reading the *News of the World*. Once father lent it to me; I had never seen it before and was appalled to see what all these good respectable Pres- byterians were lapping up, so I thanked them and handed it back as soon as I could. The main lack in the house was hot water; I badly missed my bath, as we were allowed only one a week. When I mentioned this to Miss Patton, she invited me to call round for a bath now and then at her house, and remarked that my people had 'all the solid vir- tues but no idea of comfort!'

The headmaster went round all the classes every morning to take the register and to impress them with his stern presence.

'The other day he came and more or less took my B2 French class for me. He spent some time correcting the exercises they were doing and rowing some of the boys who had done French last year. I didn't think it a very good idea, because his victims were small and I don't think they have the mental equipment to do anything perfectly. I disliked standing there listening to them being bullied and threatened with the cane. He said I wasn't strict enough with them, so I toughened up somewhat, but I hated sending boys to be caned, and was always at a disadvantage where that was the only punishment. But then, his idea was that the children should be sitting silent at their desks all the time. One morning my adorable Prep class was dutifully chanting some French verbs or phrases after me, and getting a good pronunciation, as they were still unselfconscious enough and could even manage a French 'r'. The head came in looking black, and accused them of being noisy. I stoutly defended them as politely as I could, and asked him how they could learn to speak French without practising, so he grudgingly yielded a point. Then, pouncing on Raymond, a little flaxen-haired English boy, he asked 'Do you like French?' to which Raymond answered with an angelic smile 'Yes!'

Sometimes when an older form was doing written work I had time to draw some of them, in pictures or words.'There is an atmosphere of complete peace in C6. The silence is broken only by the odd turning over of a page, or a gruff remark from Matt Lowry. Kennedy's hair falls in red wisps over his square forehead; it is darker on top where it is greased, and has a carroty band above his neck. Sylvia, don't go to sleep! Chesney and Kernohan actually look absorbed. Even Noëlle has ceased to chatter and is sucking her pen earnestly. Isabel, as usual, is proceeding methodically with the work in hand. Edna, sitting by herself, appears to be concentrating. The piano being played for the singing lesson in the assembly hall adds a run of arpeggios, changing later to 'Up with the bonnets of bonnie Dundee'.

In English classes I sometimes asked the children to try their hand at writing poetry, and this idea brought out some good results. I found that we had an angel in our midst, Kathleen, who had been at Mr Russell's school where they had time to write poetry nearly every day. This is one of hers:

'Dark and dull the wintry morning,
Raw and drowsy is the sky;

Melting drops from idle thickets
Trickle down, expand and die.'

She said it was broadcast. Molly wrote a most finished philosophical poem: 'Is school worth while?' and Roberta's was something like the grace for light. One of the boys wrote an essay on autumn in verse, and a funny little boy who didn't think he could do anything, wrote:

'The king sat on a cushion
Doin a bit of brushin,
When down come a bogey-man
An said could he give him a hand'.

The rhymes are correct according to his pronunciation. While they wrote, so did I:

'Imprisoned by the school-room wall
I watch the leaves' high whirl and fall ...'

That was how I felt, and I had no desire to bully my fellow-prisoners. I was amused by the size of some of the C6 boys towering over me as I sat at my desk in my gown looking at their puzzled faces, explaining how to do their French and wishing that they were not obliged to take it for their certificate.

I usually stayed late correcting books, as there was nowhere but a cold bedroom to do them in the house. Dear Mary Gibson usually made tea in the staff-room about half-past four and persuaded anyone there to share it. If I saw that I'd be there for a good while, I gave in and had some; indeed she'd have had us all eating up her tea if we had let her. Miss Patton asked three of us 'young staves' to tea at her house, Jean, 'young Gladys' and me, and was very kind and amusing. Gladys must have been going on to sherry somewhere, as she was waved off with 'Have great drinks!'

One evening, feeling I needed exercise, I went out for a walk, but the flatness of the fields all round and the thick mist gathering made me dislike this inland area and long for the sea.

Well, I plodded on, working hard and hoping I was doing some good. Miss Patton had lent me Damon Runyon's 'More than Some-

what', to which she had taken a great fancy. It seems to have affected
my diary style:

'As time goes on, C6 seem to grow duller and B1 more unruly.
Altogether I do not exactly enjoy this place, especially when I am
told the day before half-term that I am not suitable and will be
replaced as soon as possible. Somehow this comes as a shock, even

though I do not think so much of myself and my work – injured vanity rather than sorrow at the thought of leaving.' I came out of the head's room after school, marched into the staff-room and found Miss Patton still there, so I said rather flatly, 'Well, the head says he wants me to go, as I'm not suitable.' She looked shocked. Though she was the senior English teacher of many years' standing, she had

Kennedy

not been consulted at all; as far as I could see, nobody was, in that school. However, she was angry on my behalf, not on her own. She showed me an advertisement by the B.B.C. for monitors for foreign broadcasts, so I applied to them.

As typing was needed, I arranged to practise on one of the school typewriters with an instruction book, advancing from l,k,j,h and 'jags hash' through 'A glad lad has a gala flag' and 'A hag has had half a flask' to the heights of 'Life is a riddle; a laugh is as good as a sigh' which sounded most appropriate.

I had a bad dose of blues on Sunday evening, November 4th, so I went out. It was lovely and wild with sudden whirls of leaves, and in the black-out I had to read with my fingers the 'Erewhon' on Miss Patton's gate to be sure. She was in, and told me a weird story of elementals threatening some traveller, told to her by a Russian lady. She talked about the pension where she stayed in France, and gave me a real live pear to eat, which made me sigh for the days just over a year ago when we who were working for Mod. used to wander round Trinity Hall garden picking up windfalls. She asked if I'd ever thought of joining the A.T.S. or anything, as there might be a chance of interesting work somewhere; a young friend who had just joined had been to see her. Though not in this connection, she was rather thrilled about the new Commandos, who seemed more free-lance than the other forces, and full of initiative as well as bravery. She said the staff would miss me, which was very nice of them. I was not to worry, for more experienced people than I had given up the place, and 'We had all been teaching before. Anyway, who'd teach when there are so many more exciting things to do!' After I'd been enthusiastic about France, she said I ought to write: 'Write as you talk', which I had been told before. We listened to the news and to an amusing postscript by Alexander Woolcott. 'Do you worry?' she asked. 'I do!' The horrors elsewhere worried us all.

'*13th November.* The head told me today that he could get someone to take over on Monday. I was delighted, though doing an uncongenial job is much better if you can see an end to it. I was to ask Miss Wilson if she'd take the new teacher, and she said 'Bring her along

and we'll see!' I told the head this, but he gave me a note to her, announcing that the new person would arrive at her house on Sunday evening, though I'd told him I wouldn't be moving out till Monday;' nor did I.

'The last two days I've been totting up the beastly registers. I made a couple of mistakes, so the school secretary produced a bottle of ink eradicator and we did illicit deeds with it. The Ministry will no doubt suspect dire forgeries.'

I went on marking books, wrote out a list of work for all my classes for my successor – more than anyone had done for me – and finished about eleven o'clock.

On Monday I settled accounts, went to Belfast, enjoyed an exhibition of Maurice Wilks' paintings and followed Miss Patton's instructions to 'have a good lunch and go to

the B.B.C. when they've all had good lunches'. There, unfortunately, Miss Thompson could add very little to the original advertisement, just a few details about the work with 'a very jolly crew of all nationalities'; as she said, it wasn't their show in Belfast.

Chapter Three

'Short Intermission'

BACK IN WARRENPOINT I tried without success to buy a second-hand typewriter. Our doctor kindly let me practise on his when he was out, and I now got to the fabulous speed of fifteen words a minute, touch-typing with no cheating. I went round to see an old friend who was working in the Postal Censorship in Belfast, to which she travelled up every day. She said there wouldn't be any vacancies for some time, but I applied anyway just in case there was, or would be, a job.

I had a wonderful week in Dublin with friends, with visits to the Abbey to see Macnamara's *Three Thimbles*, to the Gate's *Caesar and Cleopatra* in the Gaiety – most enjoyable – and to the Peacock to see *Candida*. I went into Trinity, saw our kind registrar, Miss Godfrey, and had a chat with Margaret, who was still looking after everybody. Bobby Tate went past while I was busy taking a photo, but I forbore to run after him and have to explain, as one usually did, who I was. I went to Players and saw *Son of Man* by Jack White, about the youth of Jesus. Another afternoon a friend came with me to a meeting of Mod. Lang., where they debated the motion: 'That a socialist regime tends to destroy culture'. Somebody said airily that Shaw would be forgotten in fifty years' time: he might have been awakening for his generation but not for ours. Dr Sheehy-Skeffington, a favourite lec-turer (known by us as Skinny), in his summing-up, remarked in his dry way that he was sorry to hear that Mr So-and-so was as yet unawakened, and hoped that something could be done to remedy this.

I spent hours in all the bookshops, buying books for my parents for Christmas, and for myself. In the Waddington Gallery we saw prints of the Impressionists. On Saturday we went to the Avoca

Peaceful Wartime

Handweavers' show of beautiful tweeds, toys and baskets, and on to see Mainie Jellett's exhibition of paintings, 'lots of gouache, brick-red crossed with pink; horses, wooden yet expressive, cream against green waves and blue sky; bog-cuttings, black and snaky; landscapes of stone-wall country; one blob-and-cube one from her New York exhibition with very murky colours'. We also saw some stained-glass windows by Evie Hone.

It was great to get back to civilisation; even going by noisy, rattling trams was fun, swinging up to the top deck. I felt as if I'd been away for years instead of one term. In Dublin there might hardly have been a war on at all. We enjoyed such good conversations and laughed a lot; I hadn't had much to laugh about lately.

Back at home I went to our local small Technical School for evening classes in typing and shorthand. My typing wasn't too bad, though slow, but I decided I'd never want a job that necessitated all those squiggles. I had never had any trouble taking notes quickly while listening, so that would have to do.

My parents had joined the various wartime groups as soon as they were set up. My father was appointed air-raid warden for our local streets and prowled round when the sirens went at night, to make sure that no lights were showing and to warn the householders if they did. My mother went to First Aid classes in the Town Hall, brought up to date her knowledge gained as a V.A.D. in the First World War, added to it the ways of detecting various poison gases, and passed her exams with flying colours. I went to classes with her for the spells I was at home. When the siren sounded occasionally at night, she went down to the First Aid post in the corner house on the sea-front just opposite the baths – an extremely exposed position, I couldn't help thinking – and spent the time very sociably. She discovered she was a natural dab-hand at darts, and enjoyed playing. Fortunately there was never an attack or any harm to repair. Belfast, about forty miles away as the plane flies, had had terrible bombings; the docks and a station were apparently the targets, but streets and streets of small houses and their people were hit as well; 900 died 16.4.41. Only lately have we heard that the city had no protection to speak of.

My Dublin friend Honor came to stay for a week in the New Year,

Part One 'Short Intermission'

The Square, Warrenpoint on a fair day.

1942 and persuaded me to go back with her, though I was afraid I might be called up to Belfast by the Censorship. We set off with pockets stuffed with packets of tea, very scarce in the South, had a wonderful fast run in the train – G.N.R. and on coal, of course – and on arrival asked the engine-driver about his speeds: on the long straight from Drogheda to Amiens St. we were doing up to seventy. We congratulated him on the splendid run. We found Honor's brother home unexpectedly on leave from the army. I stayed nearly three weeks, as they wouldn't let me go home without a reason. I bought wool and material without coupons, and we kept buying books. I went into College a few times, and spent half an hour talking to our education Professor Fynne. Later on, Honor told me his comment on first hearing where I was teaching: 'My God – that hell-hole!' It was during the next year or so that I heard that the head had died; I was told that he had been drinking heavily – poor man – poor everyone! My mother sent the promised wire when the letter arrived from the Censorship: 'Report for duty Feb. 2nd', so I went home.

Chapter Four

Postal Censorship, Belfast

THE CENSORSHIP OCCUPIED Drumglass House outside the town, set in its own grounds with a lovely view across to the hills. I cycled out there every day and we showed our passes to the cheerful little English doorman who hailed us with 'Nice morning, ladies' or 'Turned out nice again!' or, if it was pouring, 'Soon be nice again!' without fail. Training lasted a week. There was a break in mid-morning and afternoon for a quick cup of tea, so I bought myself a huge mug decorated with pink roses. Lunch could be had in the canteen, and here I ate heart, liver and kidney with the best of them.

I found digs in the house of a rather gruff woman in the Civil

Postal Censorship.

Defence, who rushed about busily, assured me I'd have to put up with little or no hot water, and fried a meal for three of us in the evening. I was quite prepared to go along with all this till after ten days she evidently changed her mind and said she couldn't be bothered with meals. So I found myself a very small cheap room in the Ingledene Private Hotel in Ulsterville Avenue.

The Censorship staff were temporary civil servants, all women. I had some very congenial colleagues, among them Mary Irwin, who lent me a book of her husband John's poems; I liked them very much, especially the way he handled the short line with grace, economy and feeling. I was placed in the registered mail department where about twenty of us worked with two supervisors whom I privately called the cat and the dog, both pleasant to deal with. We handled only incoming mail, so there was no intrusion into letters from people we knew; any one that was addressed to a familiar name you simply handed to somebody else to read. The first thing we did on opening each envelope was to record the money enclosed.

Each of us had an official number, printed on the seals we used to close the letters. Most of them were to servicemen and followed a stereotyped formula: 'Dear Alf, I hope this finds you as it leaves me, in the pink. Here is 2/6, I hope that old censor doesn't help himself to any of it.' etc. The only codes we ever came across were obvious private ones that it seemed mean to be reading. Rarely did anyone write anything 'anti-security', but any reference to troop movements or locations or bomb damage had to be cut out with scissors, making nonsense of the news on the other side. The reputed 'blue pencil' would not have been any good against ink. Most of the work was pretty boring, and when in addition I grew tired of the smell of old bank-notes, I asked for a move to ordinary mail.

If I'd thought the registered letters were dull, the others in their near-illiteracy were much worse. I found only one really good, amus-ing, affectionate letter from a photographer father to his married daughter, describing his efforts to buy clothes and to rescue his long johns from falling out of the parcel – all sorts of funny little details. After a couple of months I did a French test; apparently my degree was neither here nor there! I translated a charming letter from an

old lady to her 'Chers Enfants', and the test was solemnly sent to
London for checking, after which I am glad to say they awarded me
an A. Alas, I don't think I had more than half a dozen letters in
French all the rest of the time, but they were interesting ones.

However, at least the spelling and odd expressions in the letters
were often entertaining, what with 'enevoples', 'did you answer anti's
letter?' and 'He lives in a bunblow'; people could be 'in hosiptal with
puneoma' – or 'nui Monia' or 'yellow joinders'; someone was knitting
a 'balicarver'; another was visited by the delightfully-named 'farewell
lady' or 'taking the baby to the clinic to be humanized' (yes, really!)
while some other couple 'damped the loons on Thursday night' (they
were twins). I liked the request 'Send me a optha of yourself', and
the comment 'oni swar qui mali ponce'. 'I hope I will can do it nice',
and 'You won't can help it', said a Glaswegian, and an Aberdonian:
'It's a fine and shortsome seeing everybody coming in and out'. I
thought 'off-minded' was good, for 'absent', presumably, and 'yafle'
for gobble. 'He frit me to death' was new to me and 'I nearly dropped
an egg (dried)'. Odd punctuation gave an ominous sound to 'Is Pat
still killing rabbits, look after yourself in the black-out'.

As we were already holding up the mail, whether letters were
actually picked out for reading or not, work went on seven days a
week, so our rest days varied. On my birthday, the first one I'd spent
away from home, as it had always been in the holidays, it was very
dreary having to work on Sunday from ten till six. However, Patricia,
an old friend, had called with a present of good drawing paper and
pencils; I'd had letters from home with money, and a greetings
telegram from my parents on Sunday cheered me up a lot.

I was writing to Maeve in Cork 'When Laura's away or, as so often,
on duty in school when I'm free, I'm stuck among a lot of old fogeys
who hardly talk the same language, or among young fogeys who aren't
much more use, are not living in exile and have no wider view of
life than that obtained from living in Belfast. I'm afraid of getting
set in an attitude of mental snobbism.'

Occasionally I got away for a week-end. On May 2nd I went home
by train, collecting Laura at Lisburn. It was a glorious summer day,
the country drowned in a fine-weather haze, with some wind. In

Laura at the Mill-dam near Warrenpoint.

Warrenpoint we went down to the baths, which were not open yet, climbed in and went down for a bathe; the water was only 53°F. After tea we cycled to Rostrevor and rode up the Fairy Glen to the derelict mill, where we sat on the high broken wall, basked in the sun and talked, watching the water-boatmen skating over the water below. Then we found the track and walked up through the plantation between waves of lovely young larches. The sun was warm on our backs and drew up an earthy, resinous fragrance of spring and summer mingled. Fairly high up the mountain we had a fine view up the valley leading towards Hilltown. As we talked, I felt, 'Things seem to fall into proportion much more when you discuss them in the sun and wind. Living in dull cities is shockingly bad for me.'

On Sunday morning, after a late night talking, we were woken by the siren and heard my mother departing for the first aid post; however, there was no harm done. Laura and I rode round by Moy-gannon to the Mill-dam, quite a big lake beautifully half-screened by young willow and alder leaves, like a Corot. Laura was leaning along a sloping tree like Ophelia. Several swans took off from the lake with a curious whirring, scraping sound.

Part One Postal Censorship, Belfast

Back in Belfast, I felt cooped up, depressed by the war, disgusted with dictators and not particularly enchanted with any government. 'The state is only a mechanism to ensure the organization of individuals, and if in this process it tries to crush any section of the population, or stifles the happiness or creativity of any citizen, it spoils its own wholeness and reality. But how can a mere mechanism have wholeness and reality? Here the state is being personified all over again, rather in accordance with the idea of Jules Romains, who saw the community as being equal to the sum of its inhabitants plus something extra.'

At work, I read as fast as possible most of the time, to make the hours go and the day seem to mean something, if I could clock up in my mind so many letters dealt with. All the same, I couldn't resist jotting down quickly the more extraordinary names, such as Flippance, Milk, Piggins, Saoul (Drunk?), Softly, McCluggage, Winks, Venus, Purple, Malatratt, Yells, Gotobed, Twist and Cowmeadow. Place-names too, especially the English double ones, fascinated me, for instance Middle Wallop (quite near where I lived later on), English Bicknell, Thorpe-le-Soken and Hatfield Peverel, where a future friend lived. Some of the Irish place-names were even better: Lisnawhiggle, Favour Royal and Cavantillycormack. One week I dabbed down a tick on either side of a line, under 'Men' or 'Women' for the use of postscripts, and found one in each 2.6 letters from men and one in every 3 letters from women, thus disposing of the myth that only women went in for postscripts, for what that's worth.

The staff fire-watched in small groups. My turn came round twice while I was there, but luckily there was never anything to do but be sociable. The place was a school in peacetime, so we slept in wooden cubicles all down a long dormitory. I was with six others, including Mr Barnaby, who kindly made tea and cleared away. We played darts for a while and I was greatly diverted.

'Mr M. told our fortunes. He had evolved his own technique for card fortunes and had, he said, told his landlady's in London, which turned out to be partly true. He was telling his own on the sands on the south coast when a man from a show noticed him and asked him to work as his fortune-teller, rigged out in Arab costume in a booth, where he made ten pounds a week sometimes. He told me there would be the death of a friend. (This I remembered particularly in the light of what followed.*) Then there would be something to do with a sailor and an airman; then a foxy-cum-fairheaded man to whom I would become engaged, and some money and letters. First he read our cups, then read the cards and ended with fixing a bed of six cards together; mine defeated him by having a death across it every time. The others had a few family quarrels and a death in Miss McC's; she was a very responsive subject and was quite depressed about it. It doesn't seem to have worried me unduly. But then of course, they told us yarns about a ghost, and just as I was falling asleep, the hot pipes started making weird clanking noises that sounded just like an old man coming along opening and shutting the doors. I was scared as anything – nice fire-watcher!'

The second time I was with Mrs Rothwell, Miss Phillips, our nice doorman and others. Mrs Rothwell, from Scotland, said she'd lived twenty years in Dublin, then moved to Belfast and had no regrets; people were very kind to her when her husband died. She and Miss Phillips thought people in Dublin examined you when you got on to a tram much more than they do here. I hadn't noticed any difference; of course all winter here you can hardly see who, or what, is getting in or even sitting beside you in the black-out.

I was enjoying J. B. Priestley's 'Rain upon Godshill', largely on Arizona and a lecture tour of American universities and towns. His reactions to campus life were very different from André Maurois'. There was a lot about time and dreams, which sounded almost the more real part of his existence. I had read only *The Good Companions* and *English Journey*, both very good in their different ways.

At Whit weekend I went home and we had Honor and Laura to stay. We walked over to Rostrevor and looked in at Miss Ross's lovely house and garden; there was even a balcony with a view of the sea. Next day, after picking gooseberries, we cycled to Cranfield, sheltering now and then from fierce thunder-storms. As we were too cold to bathe when we arrived, we did 'keep fit' exercises instead. I had been

---

* See page 35

Lurigedan, Co. Antrim

going to the 'Health and Beauty' class at home between jobs and found it very energetic and enjoyable. We discussed our jobs, and Vera Brittain's *Testament of Friendship* and agreed that Winifred Holtby sounded a delightful person. Otherwise – 'What have I been reading lately? – Very little, much too little: mind going to rust. Very pleasant to have them both around!' I was very lucky in that my parents made them welcome, especially my mother, who enjoyed our invasions as long as I was able to rig up beds for us.

Chapter Five

Life Class, Cycling, The Flat

THERE WAS A LIFE DRAWING CLASS in Belfast Technical College long before it developed its own College of Art. At last I sum-moned up the courage to go to it on Thursday evenings, and found that it had a very good teacher, an Englishman.

After a few weeks, I noted down 'On the 28th, Laura and I were slightly late. Mr Mansfield looked up and waved us into the little inner room where Trudi and two others were doing fifteen-minute studies of the male model. I never drew so quickly. Once he limited us to five minutes. He seemed to approve of my efforts – better write it down or I'll think later that it was imagination – and said 'You're doing very good work, drawing in a nice free way, getting plenty of movement'. Later on he said I must select lines more, emphasise the significant parts: otherwise my drawings would tend to be records rather than drawings proper. Quite right, of course and I'm glad not to be let rest on my oars. My standards have risen enormously and my drawing must try to catch up with them. He does it all so easily, sometimes standing at arms' length, left hand hovering rather like a fencer's.'

He was slim, neat and quiet, not very tall, with a sense of humour. I gradually got used to having somebody looming up to look at my efforts; if he drew, it was always down the side of the paper in a few expressive lines.

That evening I went home with Trudi and met her mother. They were German Jewish, and after the father's death they had got out of Bavaria just in time. In Northern Ireland they had gone through a pretty gruelling time in domestic work, which was all that was allowed for refugees at first. They had then been allowed to find a flat in town, and Mrs Neu had managed to buy a sewing-machine and do dressmaking. Trudi, who had trained in art school at home, designed and made the most ingenious toys for one of the big shops; her label, 'A Trudi Neu Toy', was clever in either pronunciation. I watched her dressing dolls in national costumes. Their rooms were lovely.

'Trudi's smells of paint and creative work and is decorated with water-colours large and small pinned to the walls and an Egyptian walking along the side of the wardrobe. We had tea and biscuits, cress and chocolate spread, and talked about Friends' School; they know Mr and Mrs Douglas well, as they are on refugee committees. We listened to the news and I wondered how they felt about Rommel, and about German towns being bombed by the British; were they not torn in two very often? They said 'Well, that is the only way to bring the war to an end', so they put up with it somehow.

On June 6th, Laura and I set off from Lisburn on bicycles for Dromara, Co. Down, on a hazy fine day. We managed to buy half a pound of margarine without coupons in the post office-cum-grocery-cum-drapery in Kinallen, and were handed half a pound of cheese,

It's a long way to Ballynahinch.

32

with a gracious air, in Dromara; these were a great help. We went round and up Slieve Croob but not to the top, because Laura put her foot down a rabbit-hole and fell quite drastically. There was a lovely light across the country that evening – sun flaking and shivering through a screen of ash-trees and sliding over the hills in great patches, showing them up. The flowering broom grew into huge bushes and hedges and looked heavenly; Laura, from Cork, was delighted with it as she had never seen it growing wild.

The youth hostel was rather scruffy, but the wardens got a good fire going in the evening and we all sat round it. Some people sat up till one o'clock and kept us awake. The bunks were made of sacking fixed on wooden frames, and we were cold all night as we hadn't asked for more blankets and a freezing wind was blowing in straight from the hills, so we didn't get much sleep.

Next morning, tired and disgruntled, we set off up and down a magnificent switchback road southward, with the sun coming out and going in. We thought we were on the Ballynahinch road, but stopped about two o'clock and asked an old fellow where we were. When he said 'About fifteen mile' from it, we made for Castlewellan and Newcastle instead. In Newcastle we had a good meal of eggs, sausages and GOOD coffee! The place was as busy as ever with trippers and American soldiers. After a walk along the sea, we rode northwards along the coast through Clough and Seaforde to a nice house with a glorious garden and rhododendron avenue which we explored. We went on to Ballynahinch, where we had tea at the local Temperance Hotel where we were allowed to eat our own food. We had an interesting chat with a lorry-driver with an intelligent, thin, crinkly face and nice grey eyes, who told us all about the lorry trade, where building was going on and where bombers and all sorts of things were to be seen. When we suggested that we might be spies, he only laughed; but we might have had good memories and told all this to the wrong people. He got 1/9d an hour extra for night or Sunday driving, and often went to Derry.

On we went to Lisburn, with a stop for each heavy shower and one when Laura's cape caught in her chain and two youths, also hostelling, stopped and undid it for her. We actually seemed to be cycling up hills that they walked, which surprised me no little. We were pleased to have spent a week-end hostelling at last, and I went back to Belfast not even feeling very tired.

A fortnight later we met Miss Patton in Belfast, went to the Allied Artists' Exhibition with her and caught up with the news. Laura and I took the train to Larne, cycled along the coast and stayed at the Cranny Falls hostel. At Cushendall we had a lovely icy bathe, pic - nicked on the shore and contemplated a bright yellow field of rape against Lurigedan rising dull-coloured in the distance. We went on up the road to Trostan to the thousand-foot contour, forked left and went down Glenariff, which was not being kept up for tourists then but was still the most beautiful of the Glens of Antrim, feathered with trees and high thin waterfalls. We got back to Cranny Falls, ate a hasty snack standing, like the Children of Israel, and fled for the train, making Larne in an hour and a quarter, with ten minutes in hand, and finished our meal in the train.

I was by then very tired of living in the hotel, with nowhere to take anyone; my room was too small and depressing and the lounge was, of course, full of residents and their visitors, especially at week-ends. I shared a table with Miss Cassidy, a kind old soul, but could have done without company when I was tired in the evening. Then they were putting up the prices, so I decided to look for a flat. I searched about and had a big disappointment over one flat in a dear little railed-off street, Mount Charles, which my father had always liked because his mother had lived there for years. Then someone told me to ask Mrs Kerr in 83 Malone Avenue, a nice quiet street, and she agreed to let me the two rooms on the second floor. They had partly-sloping ceilings which I liked. The back one made a fair-sized bedroom and the front one was sunny and quite big, for a sitting room.

On my last night at the hotel I found cockroaches on the floor when I was pulling out suitcases and packing; I didn't get much sleep after that. I spent the week-end at home gardening and swimming, and went back to Belfast with our famous camp-bed and its 'biscuits', used by my uncle in his early days in Uganda, and all the basic odds and ends. I carted all this by taxi from the station, called for my luggage at the hotel, helped by dear Miss Cassidy, and installed myself at Mrs Kerr's.

It proved to be a very good move. I was delighted to have my own flat to which I could invite my friends. Old Mrs Kerr was a most kind and helpful landlord, who cheerfully allowed me to use her kitchen and bathroom; we never seemed to get in each other's way. She had a nice girl who lodged in her spare room; she worked in a bank and went home at week-ends. Mrs Kerr's granddaughter Jill, aged eleven, had lived with her for many years since her parents' divorce; she was a sturdy little girl with short wavy fair hair, grey eyes, a squarish face and pale, fine skin. She was most intrigued by my setting up the flat and watched, without ever being in the way, while I Darkalined the floors and painted lard-boxes for book-cases and cupboards. I brought a little upholstered chair, a few cushions and a card-table from home; I didn't want to buy furniture, even second-hand, as I didn't know how long I would be in Belfast.

One weekend at home three friends and I took a visitor of theirs, Cecilia Dippenaar, up the Rostrevor mountain. She had come from the Orange Free State to finish her medical degree in Trinity and return to join her father's practice. We had been friendly in Hall. It was a lovely afternoon and coming down we went tearing through chest-high bracken. I remember Cecilia's delight at knowing there were no snakes and plunging after us through the tall growth with happy abandon.*

I went to the Opera House to see Emlyn Williams' *The Light of Heart*. It was a bad audience, mostly forces, with standing room only; that was not too bad until the interval, when they all barged past me rushing for the bar.

Censorship work was like ploughing through unsalted porridge. I often thought it would be a splendid cure, or punishment, for the inquisitive. In August I was writing to Laura who was at home in Cork on holiday: 'The point is, if I feel like this now, what will I

---

* This fine girl died with all other civilian passengers when the Germans sank the Union Castle Liner, *White Castle*, off West Africa on 14 November 1942.

feel like buried in a girls' boarding-school? It's too like 'East Wind on Friday'. One of the services would be worse, I imagine. If I knew I could cope well with teaching, I wish I could get at it; I feel I learnt a lot in my first effort. I KNOW that Rosa (a colleague) is wrong when she says 'Stay where you are and go on drawing your pay'. I'll be unemployable if I stay here much longer. I fear I'll have a bad dose of spring fever next year, shut up indoors. As someone said lately 'The only thing to do is just give up feeling till after the war to preserve one's sanity!'

Chapter Six

Cycling Tour in the West

O N AUGUST 26TH Laura came north and we set off, in haste as usual, to catch the train to Enniskillen, where we put up at the very comfortable Railway Hotel and had a meat tea. We heard the piano being well played and found a Scottish airman at it. After a while we began talking and his friend, a Londoner, came in. They were fed up with being a year 'in this dump', with half-cooked food in their camp and no aircraft. We discussed drinking; they had only begun drinking Guinness over here. They didn't like to see women drinking, and said it was done in a more sociable way in England, with a sing-song, not in dead earnest to get drunk, as here. Against that I cited McLoughlin's well-run pub at home, not that I'd ever been in one myself except once with a friend in England, but I would have agreed that women didn't go into pubs here. We discussed patriotism, and the idea of Laura's joining up – she had a sister in the WRNS – but they were dead against it; then Yanks – 'They go mad on drink, the black troops even more so' – and smuggling: they had to get a pass to go over the Border, but identity cards could be borrowed instead! After the raids on Glasgow, the cards of those killed had been used. The intelligence service, coding and decoding, was supposed to be interesting, giving one inside information on the conduct of the war. Apart from the general impression of cynicism and overpowering boredom, it was an interesting conversation.

Next day we were vastly entertained by a kind of circus procession of American soldiers on horseback – trying to be cowboys? – who trailed up the main street and back again; they let out whoops of delight at our fairly unobtrusive cycling rig-out, unlike the natives, who were not impressed. We rode round the north side of Lough

Erne, eventually reaching Boa Island, hot and tired, and paddled out to a boat in which we picnicked and camped for the afternoon, sunbathing with towels draped over our heads. When we left, we stopped at a house for a drink of water and saw a huge open fireplace with a lovely turf fire and a big iron pot hanging over it on a chain.

We rode on, seeing other beautiful views of the lough from time to time, and so in dusk and dark by the river road to Ballyshannon. The town looked very well by lamplight and afterglow and the moon hung yellowish-red over the wide river, adding a long, broken reflection. We spent the night in a nice, spotlessly-clean room in the Imperial Hotel, where the dining-room was decorated with china swans, glass bells, Belleek ware and a set of blue glass castor-holders.

In the morning, while Laura was having a bath and I was waiting for mine, a wee lad walked into the room. When I said hello, he looked scared and disappeared. Later we saw photos of a sweeping curve of thirteen children, the youngest of whom we saw crawling half-dressed down the stairs. Down the street we were amazed at the architecture of the National Bank, a mixture of what Osbert Lancaster would call Scottish Baronial and a Wren-like tower. We went on to

Laura Sketching.

Thatcher near Rossnowlagh, Co. Donegal.

a place near Rossnowlagh where Laura wanted to paint. I took a photo of her standing up on a ditch, sketching away, and one of a man thatching a cottage with wheat straw, pegged in with bent withies; he said it had to be re-done every ten years. We had our picnic nearby and gave some butterscotch to the children of the house, who at first had fled in panic to the door, but recovered.

At Rossnowlagh we rode along the strand and swam in luke-warm yellow waves. After that, while we were sitting on the ditch having a cup of tea, everyone who passed was very chatty, asked where we were from, where we were going, or, if they had nothing else to say, asked as they walked past 'What do you think of the war? Will it soon be over?' A rather villainous looking man, in a leather waistcoat and a torn shirt showing two large triangles of brown back, came along with a big pollock and asked whether we had any cigarettes. Another man came along in a car, 'so this lad shouts at him for a lift, and then stops to talk to a couple of haymakers in the field while the car waits. There is a lot of chat about 'that tanner'. If the driver protests, that doesn't matter; business deals can't be rushed.'

We moved on through Laghy and Ballintra by hilly, curvy roads edged with fuchsia and ash-trees, a very pleasant, intimate landscape with glimpses of the sea. Past Donegal town we came to Inver, and went to the Drumbeg Hotel, where I had stayed with my father, for a meal, and as it was nearly dark we decided to stay the night.

Going up to change, Laura was stopped by one of the girls to be told that some chap from Sligo wanted an introduction; this caused us much amusement. We had a wonderful supper of hot salmon-trout and cucumber, with bowls of potato salad and beetroot, brown bread and gooseberry jam, ginger-bread and tea with lump sugar and cream.

'The hotel looks as pleasant and comfortable as it did last July. Nasturtiums on the table look startling against the blue ivy-patterned wallpaper. The doors and windows are white, and the windows uncovered and blazing out into the night seem strange after the black-out, and to be letting out too much of the house. We went out on to the terrace, to find that our bicycles had been put away for us, and suddenly saw the moon, incredibly yellow, over the distant trees.'

In the morning, after a marvellous breakfast of plums and cream and bacon and eggs, we explored the garden and grounds and saw a big pond covered with water-lilies. We set off in a shower about one o'clock for Dunkineely, and went on by a very hilly road in damp heat under a grey sky to Killybegs, rather a small, grubby village than a town. On and on and up and down went this road, and the sky never cleared all day so, though there were marvellous views, it was no good for sketching or photos. Each time we toiled up a series of hills, we had to shoot down again to sea-level and begin all over again.

Between Dunkineely and Carrick, we decided that no road would ever have terrors for us or our bikes any more. In one place we looked down to the left over a grassy precipice at haymakers far below, moving about in a detached world. One young fellow in a field by himself was mowing in a white singlet and dark trousers with a black beret on the back of his head. He waved up at us and wanted to know if we had any matches. He moved very quickly with great sweeps that left the hay in uneven lines.

Glencolumbkille – next land America.

Peaceful Wartime

Further on, we saw a man padding down the road barefoot, and later, a woman also without shoes. It was the first time I had ever seen adults barefoot, and it was a long time since I had seen children down the west coast in bare feet. I was fascinated by the thatch on the cottages and the way it was put on round the chimneys; sometimes there was no chimney at all and I wondered how they could just have a hole in the roof without the thatch catching fire. I drew some of the chimneys and non-chimneys.

When we had gone inland from Carrick for seven miles and were getting to the end of the south coast of Donegal, we enquired for Glencolumbkille but heard there was no village of that name, just Cashel, which was not on my map. We asked the priest where was the Glen Head Hotel, but he directed us to the Glen Bay, which was grander than we wanted. We rode half-way to Malinmore nearly in the dark, saw nothing but cottages and desolation, and asked an old man coming back from fishing, who told us to go back and turn right. At the door of a two-storey house we asked if this was a hotel. The girl who had opened the door with a candle in her hand looked a bit blank, but they gave us a room containing two double beds and eleven holy pictures, two of which were prints of well-known ones, one of the Madonna and Child and one, rather like an El Greco, of the Deposition. The place was clean and the beds hard but quite comfortable. We wandered about downstairs in darkness and confusion for a while till the girl Norah brought us an oil lamp, by the light of which, at ten-thirty, we ate a great meal with two fried eggs each and strong tea.

We then moved to the sitting-room, papered in a large jacobean design and full of pictures, with a row of photographs of the Pope and lesser notabilities along the top of a chest, and others framed in shells on the walls. There we met two sisters who, we thought, were national school teachers, very anxious to improve their Irish; one of them was engaged in ploughing through a book of stories of Cuchulainn. When at last we were going to bed, I went down to get Laura a hot-water bottle; in the kitchen I found a big fat old fellow having his supper of small potatoes rolling about the table, and tea. I borrowed the iron to iron my shirt while he chatted about Chicago and about seeing a hundred girls working in a laundry there. He said he had been over there twenty years, right to the Pacific coast, in Seattle and San Francisco, working on the street-cars. I asked what it felt like coming back to Ireland after all that. 'Good; it felt good. I'd rather live here than any place,' he replied. He was like Falstaff in figure and slightly drunken benevolence; I liked him.

In the morning when we'd had our breakfast of fried egg, toast, brown bread and jam, and the people of the house had gone to mass after great fuss and bustle and cleaning of shoes in the bicycle-cum-turf-cum-boot-room, I went into the kitchen to dry the damp off my clothes and shoes. There was a big turf range, which I drew, and dozens of bunches of dried fish of some kind and bream, hanging from the ceiling. It was very peaceful and I was feeling completely at home and just about to take a 'still life' of some cups and saucers on the table and two large lamps on the window-sill when they came trooping back from church, so I didn't.

We packed our bikes and climbed round the rocks to take photos. It was very like the Breton coast, with black jagged rocks, foam and pale green and dark grey water. We rode round to Malinmore and

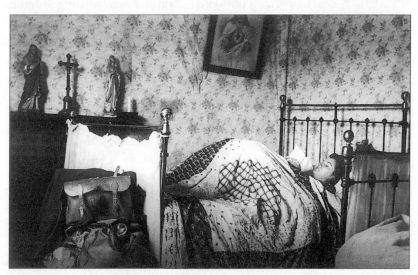

Laura in the hotel at Malinmore.

43

looked at the Glen Bay Hotel – bed and breakfast 8/6, no less – and wound our way back to Cashel. Here we posted a card, bought bread and butter, biscuits and chocolate in the one shop that was open, whose ceiling was covered with hob-nailed soles. We wound on up the road as far as a very waterfally river, probably the Murlin, where we had our lunch.

The track wound on up round a mountain and suddenly we were on the top, with a fine view each way. We kept on through moorland for some miles and stopped at a cottage to ask our way. Inside, it had a high roof with blackened rafters. The wide chimney narrowed only slightly at the top. Over the turf fire hung a wide flat pot, its lid covered with burning turf, which contained bread made from their own wheat, ground in the local mill. In front of the fire stood a griddle supporting a great slab of oatcake. The old man was very chatty; almost the first thing he said was that he had been eighteen years in America, in Seattle and San Diego, and could claim American citizenship because he had been living in Washington before it became a state. His lame daughter, who had a nice, short face, little nose and freckles, showed us some embroidery on linen handerkchiefs, very fine, which she said they considered coarse! I was wishing I could enjoy all this without needing to photograph it, but I was glad afterwards that I'd asked the old man to sit by the fire with his pipe for a time-exposure, because it came out well and is a treasured record.

Further on, going down Glengesh, we fell in with a girl on a bicycle who told us that she came from Stravally, where her mother span wool, she carded it and her brother Patrick wove it. I was mad with myself for missing the notice she said they had outside, though I was looking out for weaving cottages. She said the wool was dyed first, then spun, carded, teased, carded again and finally woven. They made about twenty yards of tweed in three months and it cost six or seven shillings a yard. They didn't take coupons, as they'd have to have a licence to do so. Glengesh was just as steep as I'd remembered it, so after all the toiling up, we all had to get off and walk down! It seemed a pity, but better than breaking our necks. At last we got on to the good surface and shot into Ardara.

We stayed at the Central Restaurant where we were very comfortably

In a cottage near Ardara.

lodged and each had a hot bath in a palatial bathroom with an enormous lock and a weak handle. In the morning, looking out, we had a view of a laden plum tree. When we looked at the register, we found that Jack White, Molinier, Trudi and two friends, and Máire Ní Eigeartaigh, Seán's sister, had all stayed there. I had a look at the cottage industries, mostly knitted socks.

We set off due south, uphill again, and over a flat upland, drab under the mist. I had tried to buy a waterproof cape like Laura's but, failing that, just wore an ancient blazer; oddly enough, I never got really wet during the ten days. In Killybegs Laura had her bicycle oiled and brakes adjusted by the engineer of the lifeboat, who said usually his main problem was filling in time. His boat, one of the biggest in the Irish fleet of twenty-six, cost £14,000, including upkeep to date.

When the rain slackened we turned east for Dunkineely, where we saw a sign of a spinning-wheel hung out and went in to find a very pleasant young woman, May Steele, daughter of the rector. She took us up to the loft where she had two looms. While she was getting out bunches of dyed wool to show us, she heard Laura say Miss Cunningham, warden of Trinity Hall in our time, and a Donegal woman herself, used to have a rug like one of hers on the sofa, and we found they had been acquainted. I bought a green-blue light shawl or knee-rug. She said she used vegetable dyes and that green was very difficult to get right; the wool had to be dyed yellow first and then blue. Blue is from indigo, purplish-pink from madder-roots chopped up and brown from crotal. The wool she used was from Scotland but not hand-spun. She gave us a lot of delicious apples that she said were windfalls, and very kindly lent me a macintosh which I was to leave for her at Coulter's, where we stayed the night. As a change from bacon and egg, we had a great supper of cold mutton, potatoes and beetroot, home-made bread, currant scones and gooseberry jam. Laura was painting when in came a man from Finaghy who told us he was a steeplejack, over here to mend the church roof. He knew Cork, painted portraits and was an expert on wirelesses, it seemed. Laura painted and we wrote up the diary till 12.30.

Next day we rode the fourteen miles to Donegal town and took the train, which started half an hour late and then went back for someone's bag that had been left behind on the platform and – to my horror, because I hadn't missed it – my precious camera. The Providence that looks after fools clearly did double duty that morning as, on the ride to the train, I had noticed my purse had fallen out of my pocket and had to go back half a mile to find it lying on the road where it fell, near my comb. In the train was an English family, a mother, two girls and two boys. The little boy of six or seven knelt on the seat and watched us solemnly with a peculiarly limpid gaze for a long time while I was writing this. The fair girl was the most striking of them and had a queer way of looking at things, intent to the point of disapproval. I tried to draw her; she had very fair skin and hair and blue-grey eyes and was very composed for her years. They got off at Rossnowlagh.

From Ballyshannon, where we had a lunch of bacon and eggs in the Royal Millstone, A. A., no less, we rode on through slight showers to Bundoran, full of trippers. We were very disappointed because the mist was over the mountains we had come to see, especially the huge ridge of Ben Bulben. By the time we reached Drumcliff Church it was dusk, so we looked at Yeats's grave and sheltered in the doorway of the church which was locked by then. We went on through Sligo, where we had an impression of lighted windows over a broad river, towards Strandhill. It was dark now, so Laura went ahead with the light. Her dark reflection on the wet road joined her outline, and it was very hard to judge the distance between us. When at last we slithered down a steep slope to the town, we had to try three places before we got a room in the Hotel MacDermott. A large homely woman opened the door and did not seem at all put out at having us roll in at 10.30. She gave us a grand meal of the usual, as we were fearfully hungry by then. We had a funny room with some of the windows opening on to the passage.

It was a beautiful morning with a stiff breeze and gorgeous breakers on the strand. Bathing was not allowed: the red flag was up. We set off for Sligo with a great view of Knocknarea on our right and Ben Bulben, now cloud-free, over the bay to our left. On the way we met an old clergyman who passed the time of day with us and said he was eighty-six; Brown was his name. Hearing that Laura came from Cork, he said his son had been in the bank there. He recited two short poems for us, on time and life:

'When I was a babe and slept, time crept;
When I was a youth and bold, time strolled;
When I was a man time ran;
Now I am old and wise, time flies.'

The other was:

'Life, we have been long together
Through pleasant and through cloudy weather;
'Tis hard to part when friends are dear,
Perhaps 'twill cost a sigh, a tear;
Then steal away; give little warning;
Say not goodbye, but in some brighter clime
Bid me good morning.'

Then the dear man sent us on our way with his blessing.

We cycled out then to Lough Gill, which looked very beautiful with cloud reflections on the water. Laura sketched and I took a photo, before racing back to catch the bus to Dromore West to save ourselves sixteen not very inspiring miles. We rode the five miles out to Easky, coming in by the hill down past the rectory; the plastered wall and sea-withered sycamores looked familiar from our family visits many years ago. The first person I saw was Jim Devany at the shop door, so I told him who I was. Then Kitty appeared and we brought our things up to the big double room. 'I went down to see Mrs Devany herself and got a great welcome. It was lovely to see her again looking the same as ever since twelve years ago. Kitty seems fatter and better looking; her hair is nearly white and not at all fuzzy but nice and soft. They have an Aberdeen called Nero who is very cute and will go out with anyone who is staying in the hotel but takes no notice of people who are there only for a meal.

'Before supper we walked most of the way down to the sea and back. We had steak and kidney, potatoes, salad and beetroot, bread, and blackcurrant jam in the big orange-pink glass bowl just as it used

48

Lough Gill, Co. Sligo

to be. Jim came up and chatted as we ate, and so did Kitty as she brought things in. We spent the evening pottering round the shop talking and hearing about the various lots of people who had been here since 1930, the year of our last visit. Mrs Devany amazed me by telling me of my playmate young Jim's tale of woe to Mrs Eaton all those years ago that he was in love with Nan (my name then). Luckily I never suspected this devotion for a moment and enjoyed tearing round as an honorary boy a couple of years younger. They seem to have had some lively bunches of lads staying, who played various instruments far into the night. They have as a resident for the fishing season – February to November, though the best time is July and August – a retired naval commander, 'a real old bachelor', who dislikes women and is deaf. He sits in the drawing-room, a nice sunny room at the back, where his boxes of flies and books on fishing are kept, not to be moved; he sleeps in the room off that. He darns his own socks, too. Otherwise they haven't had many people this year. The bathroom is new, with a fine bath. It is pouring rain tonight.'

It was fine when we woke about nine. After breakfast of porridge with creamy milk, bacon and egg, we packed and went down to bathe

49

Peaceful Wartime

The Devany Family,
Easky, Co. Sligo.

Cottage in Co. Leitrim.

off the pier. It was a glorious day with a stiff breeze blowing and the water was pretty cold but clear with a full tide. Afterwards we pranced about doing exercises, hoping to get a bit sunburnt, and took a photo of a fishing-boat against the sparkling sea. We rode back and, after a brisk walk in the other direction, enjoyed our lunch of chicken and bacon and stewed apples that I had helped to peel, and coffee and a bun, finishing about four. I took a photo of the family under the forty-year-old apple tree, which had a wonderful crop, and was given some apples. We settled up – it didn't seem much – made our farewells and resolutions to come next summer and learn to fish, and departed.

The bus for which we hadn't waited caught us up only a few miles from Ballisodare. The conductor waved most jovially at us from the back as we pedalled hard up a long hill. Fortunately it had topped the rise before we fell off puffing and walked up the rest of it. We had tea and listened to songs on the radio at the Swiss Restaurant (why on earth Swiss?) and rode on towards Dromahair. We asked the way often, as the roads were many, winding and crossing, and rode on in the dusk through a most fascinating country with a wave of weirdly-shaped mountains on the left behind us, which seemed to keep the same shape even though we changed direction often. I had no idea that part of Co Sligo and Co Leitrim were so beautiful or so enchanting in the half-light. Nothing seemed to go wrong: we took no wrong turning, bumped over no pothole, as the road was smooth white clay all the way; we managed to avoid the almost invisible donkeys standing quietly in the road here and there, and the even less frequent people. We sailed up hill and down dale at a fair speed for a long time by starlight and afterglow that silhouetted a big tree or a thorn-bush now and then. At last when it was almost as dark as it was going to be, we came into the village, guided by a local man on a bicycle, and arrived at the Abbey Hotel, a most delightful place, where we had a grand supper – 'Will you have half a dozen eggs?' – (instead of one a week on the ration). Our room was a lovely big one with two most comfortable, springy double beds and a basin with really hot water. After our thirty-mile run, we went to bed at a reasonable hour, though I lay awake for some time.

On the last day of our tour, when Laura woke me at eight, it was

Ben Bulben, north of Sligo Bay.

pouring rain, but the sun soon came out and we hurried down to breakfast. We bought bread, butter and chocolate in Dromahair and sallied forth by the road along Lough Gill, passing various lovely old rectory-like houses and gardens. We had a great view of the lake, ruffled by the wind, with long streaks of foam curved across it, which we could see better when we turned on to a little road up the mountain-side at a steep angle, really a track, leading to Manorhamilton. We photographed the lake before the sun went in. Then we had to push up the hill that seemed about one in five for a long time until we were above the peaks of the little mountains whose bases edged the lake. The blackberries were ripe and we kept stopping to eat them, and there were plenty of sloes. We passed a school where about twenty children were out playing, who cheered us as we went past. Then we came to a delicious little lake set among its own mountains, very steep on two sides, with a cottage on the far side that we thought we'd love to rent some time. My father afterwards told me about a lake that sounded just like this one, where they used to have hare drives. He was first stationed at Derrygonnelly in County Fermanagh, about sixteen miles to the north-west.

Very hungry, we reached Manorhamilton and rode on, looking for a good picnic place. We had our lunch and went on in a drizzle, with fine breaks now and then. We had no bother with the customs at Belcoo. On the way to Enniskillen we passed eight policemen at a crossroads, who afterwards passed us in a lorry, with beaming smiles. When we reached the town I was pretty wet and so were Laura's feet, so we had a good meal in the Railway Hotel and a hot wash before catching our train to Belfast. We had an hour's wait at Omagh so I wrapped myself, rather wet, in the new shawl and snoozed. At last arrived in Belfast, we repacked our bicycles and rode to the flat in pelting rain. Mrs Kerr didn't seem to mind a bit being roused at midnight to let us in, and made quite a fuss of us. We made some porridge and Laura stayed the weekend while I worked on Saturday afternoon and Sunday. Our friend Maeve came to see us and we had great crack hearing about her new Civil Defence job and telling her all about our tour.

Chapter Seven

Friends and Decisions

EARLY IN OCTOBER Honor came to Belfast for the week-end and Laura and Maeve came round to the flat. We pottered round bookshops, and Honor had her first sight of American soldiers, a new species to her. I was by then thinking of trying to get a job in Dublin in teaching, library work or the Permit Office.

At Hallowe'en I went to Dublin to Honor's family. A middle-aged couple on the train were delighted with the lights in the windows and the stations, after three years of black-out. Laura had brought Maeve to spend the week-end with her family up from Cork, and we

Honor, Maeve, Mary, Jill, Rosa and Laura reading cups in the flat, 83 Malone Avenue, Belfast.

all met for coffee in Mitchell's. The four of us enjoyed old haunts: lunch in the Country Shop; supper in town after seeing Edwards and MacLiammóir in *The Man Who Came to Dinner* at the Gaiety; walking the length of the West Pier; sitting up talking till all hours.

I went on feeling very restless. For weeks I scanned the *Times Educational Supplement*, but from what I heard, the choice seemed to be between big schools with thirty to forty in a class and small schools with poor pay and prospects. I wanted to be part of the war effort, which meant giving up the idea of working in Dublin. I greatly valued my present freedom of movement, choice of leave dates, weekends at home now and then and the company of friends in my flat, and I wondered if the interest of a new job and surroundings would make up for these. I had been nearly a year in a job without post-war prospects, and had no wish to be left high and dry afterwards.

Honor came north again in December and the four of us met for meals out and Christmas shopping, and went to a Russian film, *Natasha*, about Red Cross nurses in the front line. 'Very realistic film: the pinging or whipping of bullets in the dust or snow near a person is a curious sound.' Their broad-cheeked faces with an expressive upturn to the upper lip reminded me of Trudi, whom I'd taken for Russian, with her fair hair, when I first saw her at the art class. She and several other friends joined us for a cider supper at the flat, which we had decorated with holly and fir and paper streamers. We finished with tea and Laura read our cups with her usual convincing air. Trudi had to go at 10.15 because of her curfew rule.

I enjoyed Christmas at home as usual, and in beautiful weather. My father had had to sell the car some time after our 1941 trip, as petrol was so scarce. He had bought a bicycle at the age of 69, not having ridden one since he was a young man, and cycled to Newry, and once a week to Dundalk for butter, bacon, eggs and sugar, all of which were rationed in the north. The customs men didn't object to letting through small quantities for a family's use, and got to know him on his regular trips. We thought it was most enterprising of him to make the round trip of nearly forty miles. Meat was not too scarce at home, as many of the country people used their own bacon rather than what they called butchers' meat; my mother said she would have missed butter far more, as the ration was two ounces a week. All this made having visitors much easier. My mother spent two afternoons helping to run a canteen in the lower part of a big house on the sea front for the soldiers stationed in Warrenpoint, and made friends with a very nice American, Mrs Whyte.

In January I had a week's leave and took young Jill home with me for four days of it to throw stones in the sea, go for walks over hedges and ditches, look at birds and animals and read and draw in the house. Our only trouble was in persuading her to choose what she'd like to eat or do; she had been so trained to say 'I don't mind'. However, her appetite doubled in a couple of days, to my mother's satisfaction, and we loved having her there.

I joined the Readers' Union, which produced some very good books, for example *Kabloona* by Gontran de Poncins, an account of a year spent by a Parisian with an Eskimo family, and Henry Williamson's *The Story of a Norfolk Farm*. Both were vivid accounts of a new way of life, the first to a much more extreme degree. I had spent Christmas money on *The Poetry Review* and *Horizon*, for the year.

In art class I was still drawing, though nearly everyone was painting. 'Trudi does water-colours on these occasions, with the result that Mansfield sheers off.' I don't think she could have afforded to buy oils so I don't know why that was. I went home with her and discussed Picasso hoping to get some light on his painting, but she didn't profess to understand him, and couldn't see the object of his profile-in-full-face idea.

From the train at the week-end: 'Sun again, seen through rain-splashed carriage window; rows of little trees standing rejoicing; faint green beard on the purplish-red-to-brick lighted earth; flocks of white hens running to be fed; multitudes of rooks high over the ploughed fields. How could anyone be content with a town life, dispense with the liberation of spirit in the country? I can love a city as much as anyone and would not willingly do without its stimulation, fast movement, collection of different human types, shops (in which I buy very little), docks, even slums, but I don't think I could exist there for long without getting out to wild places; I have never tried to.'

Peaceful Wartime

I had escaped some time before from ordinary mail and got myself moved to the R.A.F. room.

'*February 17th.* Today Mrs R. told me I could stay in the new department. I was delighted, especially as she said she was pleased. The people here work much harder than my old lot, but when there's a break one is able to enjoy it as one sees fit. I find it pretty strenuous on the whole; I'm distinctly tireder at the end of the day but not fed-up, as I was for weeks at the ordinary mail, and not worn out by breathing stale, hot air all day. This room has a splendid view, lots of windows and quite a lot of fresh air. The atmosphere is cheerful and friendly and the boss's interest in the work is so much more heartening than the old lady's fussiness.

'I've been reading Epstein's *Let there be Sculpture*. My ideas on art are being jumbled up and stirred about, so at present I feel I know nothing and have no standards. I have at least invented a lampshade – 'leaf in the wind' shape – that softens the light from a white glare to a yellow glow. Wonderful mild fresh spring day; sweet air; positively Chaucerian. Lovely to see the light again; morning and evening I rejoice in it.'

Maeve's fiancé, Billy, a naval officer from Cork, was on embarkation leave. They came round for tea with Laura and me and then decided to go on a beer-hunt. They arrived back with a great collection of bottles and we had a peculiar mixture of food for supper all washed down by a pint. Laura and I enjoyed our beer but Maeve didn't like it much till she found she wasn't supposed to sip it and lick her whiskers. Billy rolled cigarettes for us of navy 'tickler'. We photographed the scene, with a great row of bottles to starboard. After all this, it was a bit late to go running downstairs with the washing-up, so we did it up in the flat and the others held on to me while I hurled the soapy water in saucepanfuls out of the window on to the road. Then we sat on the windowsill in the moonlight and I played the flute. We weren't noisy enough to disturb the Kerrs below; in any case, Mrs Kerr was so pleased to meet Billy in naval uniform, reminding her of her son, Jill's father, that she would not have said a word.

'*18th March, 1943.* The weather has been so wonderful during most of February and now March that it seems simply wicked to stick to an indoor job. Everything conspires to make me change. I work pretty hard, and the harder I work, the tireder I get and the more my eyelids twitch. It gives me a great deal more satisfaction to get a lot done now than it ever did in the other room; even then, I'm only average or a little above. Occasionally I can't get on with it, and say 'Well, what does it matter anyway? I do more than I used to,' but the 'average' for the room 'driveth onward fast', and I don't want to be a block on the line. It's quantity, not quality that is my aim; sheer eye-work, hardly brain-work and no physical effort, yet some days I can just about cycle home and then flop, too tired to eat. Then a pot of tea, strong and sweet, and maybe a letter to write, kind of revive me, especially on a sunny evening when I get the benefit of my window. This evening the sun is sinking in a summer mood and a cloudless sky, and gives a diffused light. There is no wind here, but in the offing it is coming in from the sea with a wonderful fresh smell of salt. The whole air is full of grace and peace.

'I thought I had given up looking for signs and wonders but really the last few weeks have been full of them. Ever since I read *The Story of a Norfolk Farm*, I have been collecting the 'pros' of joining the Land Army: natural inclination to stay out of doors; reaction from a negative, uncreative job; the example of a literary man who found such release and satisfaction in farming; the marvellous weather – all these have combined to point me in that direction. Giving up the flat and the fairly frequent visits of my friends would be a wrench, but new surroundings and a new job might partly offset that, and I wouldn't have time during the day to repine. Financially I hope I wouldn't lose very much; I wouldn't have the need or opportunity to spend much.

'As far as I can see, there is no mental work except teaching that I could do as a civilian, and a civilian I mean to remain. A post in a decent – i.e. a big – school would be a heavy responsibility, especially nowadays when the work is extra heavy, and at the moment I don't feel equal to it. Nothing will ever stop my interest in education, but one cannot be a teacher without confidence in one's suitability, and mine has been shaken. The rôle is an arduous one in itself, apart from the actual teaching, and it is not a thing one can experiment with and give up.

Peaceful Wartime

'Life on the land would be a peaceful existence in comparison. A great point is health: I cannot continue indefinitely to sit in an office feeling under-exercised yet tired all the time. I will not waste another year of my youth feeling that everything in spring and summer is happening somewhere else, and being left behind clutching at summer by shreds – weekends (when I have them) and my nine days' leave a year – when autumn is already clipping the days and leaves and the warmth dies.'

My parents were not enchanted by my decision to join the Land Army, especially my father, who of course said it was a waste of my education and did not speak to me for a week before I left. This was not very pleasant for my mother; I don't know how she put up with it. On the other hand, eighteen months ago my father had been most unenthusiastic about my teaching, which as far as we could make out then, seemed to carry a Victorian aura of governessing, to him, and I had had to go ahead and earn my living, anyway.

However, before this, during the Easter holidays Jill came down to stay with us for a while and we all enjoyed her visit. She came out in a boat one day and held an oar for a while. We made an expedition up the Rostrevor mountain on a windy, showery day. She was most intrigued to learn that you could tell whether the next rain-cloud was likely to hit us by watching the direction of the wind hurling the clouds along; we had a grand view of the skies. It didn't surprise me when she became a geographer later in life. I have a photograph of her planted on top of a high rock with a stick, gazing out to sea, looking like an explorer.

Jill at Warrenpoint.

Jill on Rostrevor Mountain.

Part Two

England: Women's Land Army
May 1943 – October 1945

Betty, Ellis, Joan, Nelly and Margaret at Idlicote Manor.

Chapter One

The Women's Land Army, Warwickshire

To join the land army, I had to ask my aunt and uncle in Birmingham to let me use their address as my English base. Although my Uncle Jack was bred as a farmer, he tried to persuade me to join one of the services, preferably the WRNS, as their daughter had, but I had no taste for spit and polish, and had not heard anything interesting enough about the services to offset all that. So from May the 20th I belonged to the Warwickshire branch and was sent to learn all about farming in five weeks' training at Idlicote House, near Shipston-on-Stour. It was a beautiful manor house, formerly owned by an American lady, and had murals of the War of Independence painted all round the dining-room walls. There were big bedrooms that slept six of us comfortably, and plenty of good bathrooms. The food was good, too. The village consisted of about eight very pretty cottages, a school and a little church.

My uniform was there for me: a short brown overcoat with shoulder-badges and green armband, a hat with a brass badge of a corn-sheaf on a green ground, corduroy breeches, green pullover, two short-sleeved shirts, three pairs of long socks, two pairs of dungarees and an overall coat, two pairs of boots, a pair of brown shoes and an incredibly stiff pair of gaiters that I got rid of as soon as possible. I never wore the breeches for work; they were too tight round the knees. We always wore dungarees, unlike the girls in the posters.

We got up about 6.30 and worked from 8 till 5 on the farm at the end of the drive, changing from one job to another every few days. Most of the girls came from Birmingham or London and had never even handled a fork or spade. For the first three days, the five from our dormitory were given four-tined forks and left in a big yard to load manure that had been trodden all winter by a herd of bullocks, on to a high trailer – about the most strenuous job on the farm. The attractive forewoman who flitted about seeing that we all had something to do and left us to it, called this 'tractor work'. When we had loaded the trailer we hitched it on to the Fordson and Eddie, a lad of few words, drove it, with some of us each trip riding on the mudguards, down a winding lane to the field where we unloaded it. Three of us kept working; the other two were soon just leaning on their forks. Nelly, a daft girl from the Black Country, never stopped working and singing, and had us in fits of laughter, though I often had no idea what she was saying in her strange accent. The men named her Tulip because her favourite song was 'I wore a tulip.' It was a standing joke that our next job would be pigs, and sure enough pigs it was.

'The pig man, Jim, is a good deal older and rather amused at us. The men are all awfully decent and helpful. There are six big pigs, thirty-five little ones and ten very small ones. Two of them were a darned nuisance when we were chasing them in as they kept escaping. The manager himself, Jim, Margaret and I took about twenty minutes to get the little wretches rounded up. It was very funny, only it was our early day off on Saturday, 3.30 instead of 5. The last two days, when we'd done the pigs and their spuds, we pottered round the rabbits and sawed wood in the barn, had a good long lunch-hour and discussed pigs with Jim, whose words of wisdom dripped like honey from the comb, slowly and patiently.

'We have a regular League of Nations here. The farm is owned by a company and managed by a Frenchman, Guissin. The agent, Lamberg, is a middle-aged little Czech, pink and cheerful. The girls are all English, much younger than I am, many of them Londoners and some from Birmingham. Each lot says to me of the others, 'Don't they talk funny!' so I make some diplomatic reply. Yesterday I met M. Guissin's father and mother and spoke to them in French, so she beamed and told me about her daughter in Paris, and how they came

Percy and Pony.

Half of Idlicote village.

to England after 1918. She is very keen on the Land Army and said if she'd been young she'd have joined it as the work is so important 'growing food for all humanity and storing up seeds for Europe after the war.' It was great to hear such a lot of good French, and so odd in the middle of the English countryside. She called her husband over, saying 'Here is a young lady who speaks French perfectly' (believe it or not). He is also very nice, wanted to know what I had been doing before and saw at once why I preferred this to such a negative, uncreative job as the Censorship. The son and daughter-in-law have an adorable child of three, Loulou (Louis) who charges about in wellingtons. He is as pretty as his father is ugly, with flaxen hair, long hazel eyes and an angelic smile for the land-girls, who make a fuss of him, of course.

'On Sunday I was just setting off for Stratford when the people from next door offered me a lift, bike and all, saving me nine or ten miles on a hottish day. I rode all round the town, had tea with tomatoes on toast and cycled back.

'We spent the rest of last week going up to the Hill Farm, half an hour's walk away when you're tired, to help Joe, aged 72, who is a hedger and a great-grandfather. We hacked away with splashin'-ooks (hedge-slashers) at a huge overgrown hedge about fifteen feet wide, chopping out elder-trees and thickets of brambles and briars; then raked up the rubbish and made bonfires. Well, I wanted to get back to nine stone and should have, after that. Our clothes were sticking to us most of the time. Apart from the heat and damp air, I enjoyed it. Old Joe was very decent to us and once I got used to his broad Warwickshire I found him most interesting talking about the old days when Lord Southampton owned the estate of about a thousand acres and 'had Irish gentlemen over hunting every season, horses, grooms and all'. He vouchsafed this morning 'A person could larn you anything because you take interest'. It was fascinating watching him laying a hedge, weaving the branches in and out of upright stakes and shoving them down with all the rough ends and bushy bits on one side to keep cattle off. I can't say I did much of it but I know exactly how it should be done. It was lovely up there this morning with a fresh cold breeze, white clouds and sun. There are a lot of

Betty, Iris, Jill and Roland weeding potatoes.

Elevator.

bean-fields nearby. This afternoon we went and singled sugar-beet till
3.30 in a vast field that I'd hate to tackle by myself.

'I have found out that we are not allowed to go away for a weekend
till the end of the five weeks; they are afraid of girls being unsettled
and neglecting their work. I haven't had time to neglect my work,
much as I enjoy the weekend – or rather, Sunday, as we work till
3.30 on Saturday. As I'll have to cart all my extra uniform back to
Birmingham in one go, I won't ask you to send much, but I would
like my West Indian sun-hat and Chaucer's *Prologue*.

'This is all very sudden about the Vauxhall; I didn't think you
were serious. I hope she has a good driver and a kind home. I'm
looking forward to hearing that you have taken a race round Ireland
on your bicycles.

'I've been to Shipston to get stamps; it's a peaceful little town
about the size of Rostrevor if the square were full of streets. Most of
the houses are built of grey and yellow crumbling limestone, some
with a lovely thatch going up and down over the windows, many of
which have sagged askew. The rest are of red brick, with a few big
Georgian and Queen Anne houses sprinkled about, and quantities of
pubs – variously-coloured Lions and Bulls. Today all the girls except
Jill and myself have gone off to make whoopee at a garden fête at
Whatcote, and it is very pleasant to have the house to ourselves. The
windows of this sitting-room (panelled in light wood up to the ceiling)
are all open, and I have a lovely view miles across country over a
new hayfield. There are cedars to the left and right, and honeysuckle
growing in at the window.'

The next letter tells of a meeting with Mary Lombard in Stratford,
where we had tea at the Judith Shakespeare café. It goes on:

'On Whit Monday sixteen of us went to the gymkhana at Shipston
on a wagon drawn by Lively, a great dapple-grey mare, decked with
bunting and with harness polished and brasses shining. She and the
dray went in for the farmers' heavy turn-out but didn't win anything,
though we all liked her the best. Six of us looked after her and cleaned
up after each rain-storm. Fred was very disappointed that she wasn't
placed in the first six. There was a children's jumping event, quite

good, and an ordinary one, pretty poor. Maybe the horses had been kept waiting too long, as they all seemed to have the jitters and refused and did every mortal thing out of devilment. I was with Jill, who rides, and we were thinking of trying to be posted together to a private farm, but I enquired of Irene, the forewoman, who divulged at last the fact that there are tractor depôts where you can be trained, and said she'd try to find me a vacancy in one.

'Last week we were singling sugar-beet, leaving one every ten inches. As it kept pouring, a lot of Warwickshire stuck to each boot and the rest to our hands. When you planted a one-and-a-half inch beet in a gap, it stuck to your thumb and laughed at you. Roland, the man in charge of field work, is extremely nice and very interesting to talk to in our breaks. He spent eight years in Canada, came back and went through the last war. He has very blue eyes, thinning fairish hair and a relaxed manner. He can be very amusing too. One day when he said he'd been very shy when he was young, the London kids piped up and asked him how he had met his wife. 'Oh', says he,

Roland, our field work instructor, guide, philosopher and friend at the Hill Farm, Idlicote.

'she was very shy too. She looked at me and I looked at her, and there it was. How does a potato begin? In the eye!'

'We did a day's transplanting on Thursday, five of us doing nearly all the work. I had no trouble getting more done than the others because I'm used to gardening. The Londoners did nothing but talk. Roland bucked them up now and then to get the field finished, but said it wasn't worth losing patience with them; they wouldn't get far in the Land Army anywhere because they couldn't concentrate. He is the chief tractorman, so I told him I wanted to specialise in that and not get mixed up in milking. He said 'Unless you want to do it, it's no good getting tied to a cow's tail, never able to get away for a day.' Part of the week we went over to the potato field and filled up gaps in the rows with seed potatoes. You never saw such heavy soil; it was hard to lever up a trowelful. When I came to a patch of pure clay I took it up and made a cross face with it, which amused the others. I spent lunch-hour making a little head, which Roland mounted in a tree-trunk.

'On Friday and Saturday I was on poultry, going round with another girl and Joe feeding geese and goslings, hens, ducks and ducklings and turkeys in pens, coops and runs all over the place. Then we set off for the Hill with four other elderly men and Joe's son Arthur, and hoed turnips. The beet was easy compared to this, as the weeds were knee-high and the mangels much lower. Next day it poured and we had to shelter for two hours at dinnertime, which gave our arms a rest. As time went on I found it a good deal easier and kept up with the rest a bit more. When they finished a row, Joe would come thrashing down from the end of mine and meet me. Arthur told me most of the geography of the county and where to cycle to see the Cotswolds. After dinner, when the men knocked off, I wandered back to the farm, saw no one and sat in the barn reading the *Irish Times* (for which, thank you) and studying a map. It felt queer to be at a loose end. Then I strolled over to the other farm and helped to saw wood and chase in the pigs. About five, I rode into Shipston and took a photograph. There was to have been a two-man-plus-accordion Ensa show that evening but they didn't turn up. We had quite a good one before, and four films at various times. The last was quite good, a serious one, but the power failed before the last reel, so somebody who had seen it told us the end.

'Next week we were still hoeing in hot weather and going down at four o'clock to water the thirsty poultry. Five ducklings came out at the weekend. I saw the first one starting. It had made a hole in its shell and was waving its bill about.

'On Sunday, after washing my clothes, I set off at half-past five and rode southwards to Moreton in Marsh, a lovely quiet little town, mostly in one long wide street of yellowish-grey stone houses with trees growing close to them down each side. It was about twenty miles there and back on a lovely switchback road.

'I went on haymaking this week, after hearing awful warnings from Arthur about how hard it was to stand on the wagon as the loader collected the hay and dropped it on you. First I was rick-building with several other girls, and two men unloading. Then I went down on the tractor, helped to load and drove up the loads. Thursday was very hot and we worked hard with a great crew, including two little London girls, Iris and Alice, from the Old Kent Road and Bethnal

Haymaking at Idlicote Manor farm, unloading an old two-horse-power wagon: Alice and Iris on the right.

Eddie and Alice

Green. Alice sang all the latest songs from the wireless; it sounded very funny on top of a huge stack but didn't stop her working like a dynamo. I got a photo of them on the stack and one of Alice watching Eddie putting a wheel on his tractor. He took her to tea with his parents one Sunday. One day she and Iris were looking over the half-door of a pen in the yard, making encouraging noises to a cow, till Alice noticed a ring in its nose, exclaimed 'Ow Iris, it's a bull!' and they fled.

'The night after the haymaking I couldn't get to sleep properly; all I did was see lines and lines of hay and feel I should be collecting it, till about 3.15. Then some of our room got up at 5.30 to milk, yapping and pounding about, so I managed a fair day's work on three hours' sleep or so. However, the afternoons were a bit slacker, as the loads didn't come up so fast. When there was nothing to do, I read the book on tractors. Percy and the other men said they wanted us four to stay on at haymaking, as they didn't want some of the others, so we had it all arranged, but Irene made the London kids swap with two other good ones, so we let it go at that.

Part Two *The Women's Land Army, Warwickshire*

'Fred the wagoner, who has been drawing loads up and wagons back all the time, fixed me with a beady eye and said 'Oi want *yow*', and was going to tell the forewoman, so I said I'd love to work with the horses (and get out of milking, which would be pure waste of time). Fred is a funny old card with a great flow of language. He has been all over the place with the army, to the Russian frontier, Constantinople, Gallipoli and the Curragh! He has a flaxen-haired boy called Ernie, with whom I've been horse-hoeing. I led Kit and killed clegs on her and he held down the big hoe. It was hard work for him and he amused me by saying 'You know, I ain't quite man enough yet for this job'. He wears an ancient battle-dress, nearly black with green faded bits; I can't make out how it began life. He told me he got bitten once when he was quite small, by one of his dad's horses that he was fetching in early in the morning. When I asked if it hurt badly, he replied 'Well, when a 'orse bites you, 'e means to bite.'

'After the first hot day on the rick, I got a shock when I saw my dark brick-red-and-brown face in the glass. My arms are also turning the required shade of mahogany. I haven't been so brown since I was in France. At least I'll look the part when I go to Birmingham for my long weekend.

'Yesterday was a red-letter day. Percy lent Jill his horse for an hour or two in the evening, as she can ride, and said I could get up on him too if I liked. Jill trotted up and down the field, first on Ginger and then on foot beside me on Ginger, and told me what to do. I thoroughly enjoyed it and didn't mind a bit when she let go. I had an idea I was scared of horses before, but for one thing, Ginger isn't very big and it didn't look too far to the ground. He is a lovely creature; Percy wanted a photo of him, so I took one of them both, Percy wearing a rosette he had won. He rides him home to dinner and we watched him cantering up the slope like the wind, wearing a very un-Wild-West navy boiler-suit.

'On Sunday I went out about ten o'clock and came through two or three lovely little villages and a big one, Ilmington, all lanes up here and footpaths down there, gardens, thatch and great banks of roses of all colours. What do you think of this? I wandered up a steep lane, looking at all the roses and stone cottages, and what should I find at the top where the path petered out but a notice in red letters on a little gate: 'Stirrup Pump Here'! It looked ridiculous, yet in Whatcote, a hamlet near Idlicote, the little church had a bomb dropped on it and was burnt inside. When I went back to the road, I came up a long hill on to a ridge that we can see from Idlicote. I'm sitting beside a signpost that says Ilmington (behind me)', Lark Stoke to the right and Campden to the left. I can see most of Warwickshire fading into a blue haze in the heat.

'Chipping Campden: here I've had to turn off the road and sit under a tree to keep cool.

'I'll hate leaving Idlicote on Friday. I've had quite enough of the hostel; it's a lovely place, but there is too much noise and scramble for meals – these people do eat quickly! I don't get much peace to read, and could do with more sleep. But I shall miss the farm and everybody on it, badly, just when I've got to know them all to talk to and got used to the various jobs. I'll want to know how the sugar-beet does that we hoed and singled, and whether it beat the wireworm, and whether old Joe gets the hedges done on the Hill, and whether the spuds we planted catch up with the others, and I'd love to see Roland's wheat harvested; it's his favourite crop, and looks fine so far.

'A lot of us went to church this morning and Jill and I stayed behind to see the vicar and look round the church. He was very interesting and told us about the Norman door, Early English arches and great thick walls that slope back towards the top. We discussed briefly the Land Army, Ireland north and south – he had been in Bantry and Belfast – Warwickshire and photography. He is pretty fat and looks and sounds rather pompous during the service but is quite different off duty; he reminds me of Emlyn Williams.

'The night before leaving Idlicote I came in nearly an hour late from work, and got rather a shock at finding two officials of the Warwickshire War Agricultural Executive Committee (always called 'the War Ag'), the County Assistant Secretary of the W.L.A. and Miss Howell, the hostel warden, all waiting to ask me to take on the job of hostel leader or forewoman of a new hostel at Ashow, over eighteen of the girls with whom I had trained. They began by asking if I'd mind not going in for tractor-driving, so I said I'd mind very much and would be terribly disappointed if I didn't. They said they were very short of good forewomen, needed one very badly for this new place, had excellent reports of my work, thought I had a pull through being older than the others and well-educated and so on and on. I said I wanted to train for tractors before the ploughing season, at latest. I then went and had my much-needed dinner, after which I went back to them, looked at the list of girls' names and found them a pretty good lot except for two lazy young idiots. They said, 'Try it for three months,' so I said 'I'll try it for two.' I was to see that each girl took a contract sheet out every morning to the farm she was working on, as they went out in gangs of two, three or four to farms within a radius of four miles, on bicycles. On Thursday evenings I was to check all their time-sheets and see that they went in to the labour officer, and pay the wages. 'They have to be at work by eight and can't leave till six, or one o'clock on Saturday, without

(What it looks like
in the advertisements)

What it feels like
(sometimes)

the farmer's permission, so I can see I'll have to be up at dawn to get my breakfast and chase them all out in time. I went in later and asked Miss Howell about the new warden at Ashow, but she knew nothing about her – talk about a pig in a poke! I'm to tell her how everything was organized at Idlicote, and we can do the same or work out new ways, so it seems I'm to have the job of training the warden as well as supervising the girls at work and in the hostel. She didn't even know the proper address of the place or how it's spelt, as it isn't on the map. All was to be revealed by the W.L.A. during my long weekend.

'I must say the eighteen girls took it very well when I told them. There are some grand kids among them, including my own room-mates. One of them, Joan, a striking-looking girl with a kind of golden skin and large brown eyes, who had been doing some pretty grim work with her aunt in Birmingham rescuing people from bombed buildings, rather startled me by saying seriously 'You've got the accent for it'. Some of them have constituted themselves my 'staunch supporters'. I might as well be back teaching, though I wouldn't want to have no responsibility at all for too long, and I couldn't very well refuse it. I do think they had a cheek to spring it on me at the last minute but then, as Roland said when I told him, they thought I'd refuse it if I had too long to think about it.

'After all that, I changed into breeches and went out riding with Jill. We did about two hours, and I was very sorry to be leaving just as I was getting the hang of it.'

'In our last week we were supposed to be hoeing in a field of potatoes so overgrown that we had to pull up waist-high weeds in armfuls. The field had been pasture and should have been fallowed or at least ploughed again before anything was planted in it; however, there was a hefty subsidy on potatoes, so in they went. It was such a job that Mr Lamberg offered us an extra twopence or threepence a row, but with Roland's approval I asked for sixpence, as we could do only three rows a day each, so I made half a crown before I moved on to horses.'

I was looking forward to working with old Fred but was with young

This envelope contained election material, as I had (and have) a vote for one of our university candidates for the Senate (Seanad Eireann). My mother forwarded it to Idlicote. Hot weather made me think of the sea. Paper shortage made me draw on old envelopes.

Ernie again, who roared ferociously at these great creatures in a good imitation of his dad. He amused me very much, having heard that I was Irish, by saying – going pinker than usual – 'You'll think I'm daft, but look, do they write the same way in Ireland?' so I explained that we mostly spoke English and wrote the same way, in case he'd got us mixed up with the Chinese. He had a good wash at night, he said, especially his feet: 'You couldn't get into a woman's bed like that', meaning, of course, a bed his mother looked after. He was a lovely kid and a great worker; since he was eight, he had got up at half-past five to go out to the field and bring in the horses to be got ready for work.

By this time I was developing quite a respectable wagoner's bellow myself and becoming a dab-hand at swatting horse-flies on the horses without scaring them worse than the flies. I went raking hay all round a huge field on my own with old Kit, aged twelve, who had ideas of her own on the appropriate working speed, stopped at the slightest provocation such as any word uttered in the field which had an O sound in it, and looked round enquiringly as if to say 'Did you say whoa?' She knew the job far better than I did, naturally, and I'm sure she was laughing at me with her ears. However, I got it done, hitched and unhitched her several times and rode her up to the field. I also did a thing I'd always wanted to do: stood up in the cart and drove another big horse, Tattling, along a downhill road, feeling like Boadicea. The last day was lovely up in the hayfield. It was hot, with a breeze, and there was a great view all across the country, blue in the hazy distance.

Official bumbledom didn't take our ration-books till the last night and gave them back with all the coupons cut out, leaving nothing for our long weekend. As my kind aunt was short of margarine, we just used the fat coupons for the next period: I never had any complaints. 'They also sent me 26 coupons for winter underclothes. I am to give up 36 out of my next book and get another ten for being an agricultural worker, which brings it level. So why do anything?' As Ian Hay summed up this sort of thing in the previous war:- 'Government round-games!'

Chapter Two

Ashow Hostel,
Near Kenilworth

IT WAS A PRETTY HECTIC TIME sorting out the first twelve girls for work in widely separated farms, and then another six, who turned out to be four when they arrived. I had very little spare time when I had fitted eighteen bicycles with pumps, bells and saddle-bags and oiled them, helped by two others; given them out to the girls and got receipts signed for them; toured the whole area on my bicycle every day up to forty miles, counting the miles I walked over the fields to find the girls; sorted out contract-sheets and time-sheets; collected employment cards and given out new ones; paid the wages and done various odd jobs.

At the end of the first week the Labour Officer, Miss Phillips, dashed up in her usual happy fashion near enough to my knocking-off time, left me a lot of work to do and informed me quite casually that I was supposed to be working in the fields from 8 to 6 every day as well as being forewoman, as 'the girls shouldn't need much supervision now' – this with four new ones just coming and seven farms, three of them new to us, to be supplied with twos and threes of girls. She might not have been so cocksure if she had managed to listen to me or seen the way some of the girls were left to work with little idea of what they were supposed to be doing and less desire to find out. At least I could give them a bit of help and encouragement. I always remember one irrelevant detail, the amazement of one very towny pair when we found a tiny oak tree just uncurled from its acorn: 'Ain't nature funny!' I asked Miss Phillips if I could go to the tractor depot instead. If she expected me to work full-time on the land as well as doing the job I'd been given, I might as well do what I'd asked to do in the first place.

The second week I tried doing both kinds of work and coped all right till Friday, when I had to spend the day chasing round getting time-sheets signed by all the farmers, who with one accord had been inaccessible on Thursday, the last day of the War Ag week.

The weekend in between, one of the girls, Sheila Day, a small rosy-faced, freckled daughter of a milkman, asked me home to Coventry to stay, and we had a very pleasant time. We meant to go to a riding-school on Sunday but it rained, so we walked round the city, looked at old buildings and the very extensive bomb damage and the cathedral, of which only the outer shell was still standing. After lunch we cycled seven miles to Atherton to see some friends of theirs who had a farm. When we got back, we pored over maps of the Cotswolds and they showed me lots of photographs and postcards of various places to visit. After another good meal we rode back to the hostel. There I had more time-sheets to dole out; I hardly had time to wash before half-past ten some nights.

Though I was glad to have the work question settled, I was very sorry to be leaving the hostel. The two Miss Turners were dears and looked after us very well, taking trouble to make our meals interesting. They said they were sorry I was being moved and I said I regretted it too and wasn't looking forward to living in hutments. I liked my two room-mates and the rest of the girls. We got on well together, Midlanders, Londoners and all, including the rather troublesome pair who had never really worked at Idlicote, found it an awful pull at first and took my efforts to 'reform' them very well.

So all that committee-meeting, persuasion and decision-making was rather a waste of energy. Miss Phillips had a girl in Leamington who wanted the job in the hostel; later on I heard the sad sequel to her half of the exchange. I was interested to hear that she did not work full-time on the land. She retired after a fortnight, saying she could do nothing with the girls; I don't know why, as they were mostly good kids and I could manage the rest. They had nothing but ructions, and it seemed that she showed little tact. 'I feel much less of a mug now, though. I hear they demanded me back, but Miss

Part Two   *Ashow Hostel, near Kenilworth*

Phillips said it was because they thought they could take advantage of having trained with me, which is quite untrue.' It was mean of her to invent that.

Instead of moping round that last weekend, I went to Birmingham to Aunt Mary and Uncle Jack. They had told me just to walk in when I felt like it, as I might not know my future movements in time to let them know, so I took them at their word, walked in at the back door as advised and was made very welcome. They were marvellously kind to me all the time I was over there; I spent many weekends there and enjoyed the luxury of sleeping the clock round on Saturday night. My uncle was then way-leave officer for the electricity board, as he knew all about the value of farm-land and the inconvenience of having poles and pylons on it. He always cooked a delicious Sunday lunch and he and I washed up. My aunt ran the wine shop in the front of the house; she would go in there when the bell pinged, serve a customer, hear part of a life-story and come back to continue the conversation exactly where she had left off, with a cleverness that never ceased to amaze me.

Chapter Three

Tractor Depot,
Leamington Spa

THE HOSTEL WAS T-SHAPED; one arm held a big dormitory for forty, arranged in two rows of open-ended cubicles with two double bunks in each. The other arm held a well-fitted wash-place. The stem of the T was a big dining-hall containing two pianos, a good wireless and a dart-board. The bunks were made of plywood with holes bored in it, on strong wooden posts. The mattresses squashed down to about an inch and a half thickness, which was all right in the summer. The ground round the building was planted with vegetables and the gardener was disgusted that they wouldn't eat the lettuces that were growing their heads off, so I said I'd take some with me for lunch. The food was very uninspiring, especially the sandwiches, though the two women who cooked no doubt did their best with the rations they were allowed. They were kind souls and tried to keep dinners eatable for those of us who were working late. Though it was hard to get any peace to read or write, we settled down fairly early at night. Everybody had to be in by half-past ten except on Saturday when it was half-past eleven; that was all very well till the tractor-drivers were working till eight or nine even at weekends and trying to get to sleep. Still, being in barracks was not nearly as bad as I'd expected. There was one warning as soon as I arrived: one of my room-mates said 'Watch your hair. We go over ours every week with a fine comb.' I promptly bought one, but luckily never found any intruders. There was a nasty moment when the poor girl who had used one of the baths just before I did was found to have scabies, but that had no dire results.

85

Peaceful Wartime

Laurie and Fred

Work hung fire for a while as the weather was rather cold and wet and we couldn't start harvesting. The tractor men and girls cleaned and painted corn-drills and reapers-and-binders in the big machinery depot just beside the hostel. Three of us spent three and a half days out on a farm using a thatch-maker that worked like a big sewing-machine, sewing two rows of stitching down the straw to make a long strip cut into nine-foot lengths. We made 155 a day and did enough to cover fifteen ricks a day sooner than the farmer expected, so he came round and gave us an extra ten shillings among us; we were very tickled. It was a pretty hot, dusty, monotonous job, though we could change places with each other. It reminded me of the Three Fates, one feeding, one sewing and one cutting off the pieces of thatch. My nails were worn down in the middle when we'd finished.

'Isn't the news good! I could hardly believe my ears the morning we heard about the invasion of Sicily; it seemed too good to be true. It's funny to be in civilization again, to see a paper now and then and hear the news, after Idlicote. The war might have ended without our hearing of it there, unless Roland had told us.'

At the weekend I cycled to Chipping Campden but couldn't find anywhere to stay till I asked a policeman, who escorted me up the street to the Plough Bakery, where I shared a room with a very nice girl of fifteen, daughter of an Air Force officer and an Irishwoman from Enniskerry, who had been brought up in India. We were sung to sleep by crickets in the bakehouse below, though we were in a room at the top of the house, with a sloping ceiling covered with beams and a plain stone-mullioned window. After a superb breakfast I rode on southwards. Unfortunately it was very hazy, so after toiling up long hills I hadn't much of a view, just long pale sheets of wheat, dark hedges and dusky blue sky. At Moreton-in-Marsh I went into the Y.M.C.A. canteen in the old market hall and was given huge sandwiches and tea. I talked to a Limerick man who had trained in the R.A.F. in Canada. 'I had to laugh when I thought of helping to feed the lions in the Y. M. canteen in Belfast with Laura and Maeve. Now I am one of the lions!'

I went to London for a most enjoyable weekend with the Scott family. Diana met me at Paddington on a sweltering Saturday after-noon but the storm broke and afterwards London looked all fresh and smokeless. On Sunday Mr Scott took us to the R.A.C. for a bathe, of all things. To get there we walked along the Strand, Piccadilly and Leicester Square. We had coffee and cakes in a room opening on to a garden full of poplar trees. Then we went to a news cinema. We had delicious meals with plenty of fresh fruit and vegetables from their garden and allotment, and red-currants from Cambridge, where Diana's sister Jean was working, analysing tinned foods. On Monday we went to a neighbour's garden to pick pears. I was taken along to climb the tree and, armed with a basket and a stick, I got most of the fruit picked or knocked off. Mr Scott was interested in farming and the country; he lent me a Cotswold map and told me of places to cycle to. Mrs Scott insisted on giving me all sorts of nice food to take back; I ate the sandwiches next day for lunch.

At last on August the 4th we sallied forth with the reaper-and-binder. I went with Ada, a very nice calm girl, and Ernest, a Pole

Laurie and the Italians ricking beans.

from Danzig. 'He is short and wide and rushes about taking his work very seriously, but is a cheerful little bloke. We were trying out a new binder and though he is good with machinery he was nearly demented because the knotter wouldn't work properly and sheaves kept falling out loose. I took over from Ada for over an hour, round and round a peculiar-shaped field that had seven or eight corners. It's quite a job getting round corners without leaving any bits uncut, with that huge contraption behind.' We used power-driven binders with a seven-foot-six–inch blade, and were sent wherever there was badly-laid corn, as we could slow down or stop and still shuffle it through the machine.

'*16th August*. From Thursday 5th I've been working overtime and weekends, which makes a fortnight with one half-day off. We work till 7, 8 or 9 o'clock, and last week did 19 hours' overtime on top of our normal 50-hour week, though we had to wait in the mornings to be collected in the van. I enjoyed going past rows of A.T.S. having inspection, with some officer finding fault with buttons or ties, especially if we happened to be sweeping by on a lorry or one of the big tractors, dressed in our greasy overalls and coloured scarves.'

'We have been working since Saturday for a Major Clark, cutting wheat, and all that time he never offered us a drink, though he and his family were clearing sheaves away from the hedge and talking to us. The second day, Ernest asked where we could get some water, but all he said was 'Oh, just go up to the house there', so we went and looked until we found a tap in the yard. After that he brought us some coffee, and got the housekeeper to make us some about lunch-time. He did bring us some lovely plums one day.

'Tractor driving is an exciting form of sport and very interesting. I'd have liked to start on something less exacting than cutting corn. They tell you it's easy, but there are lots of things that can go wrong, and ways and ways of cornering. I still find Ernie very hard to understand and so do the others. Unfortunately French is no good either. I drive a Fordson up hill, down dale, along very steep slopes and round appalling craters where they have blasted out tree stumps and not filled in the holes, and have often left roots sticking out too; all this in bottom gear with the engine roaring so that it's very hard to hear my mate yelling 'Whoa!' if we have to stop. He can't whistle, but has at last got a stick to slap on my mudguard as a signal. When the tractor's in low gear the knife works more quickly from side to side in proportion to our speed, as the binder is worked by a power-drive from the engine and, unless the crop is very thin, it needs low gear and full throttle to avoid choking the binder. We've done mostly wheat and seventeen acres of badly laid tall oats.' I didn't tell my parents that the naked power-shaft whirled very fast just below and behind the foot-plate of the tractor – talk about 'safety at work'! Needless to say, we didn't leave anything trailing near it.

'On August the 16th, all the tractors and binders in the district seemed to have congregated in the big spread of War Ag land at Three Gates. There were three outfits charging round one nineteen-acre field; really, it was like a circus. It was very hot until late in the afternoon.' There were three girls who worked with me there all the time. Joan Hosker was tall, slim and crowned with a mop of short black curls; she had circumflex-accent eyebrows, wide cheekbones and

a pointed chin. Laurie Roberts was thin, even frail-looking, with fair wavy hair, pale square face, light blue eyes and a wide mouth full of jokes. Margaret was quiet and dark, with long hair tied back, hazel eyes and a gentle voice and manner. Laurie, Margaret and Ada, too, were married to men away in the forces, and lived in their own flats or in digs, as did Joan. They all came from the Birmingham area and Joan and I used to travel by train sometimes at week-ends later on. They were quite different from,

Ellis and Fordson at Three Gates

and much more interesting to talk to than the girls in the hostel, who used to amuse me by getting up early to spend time making up their faces for work. One girl in our little half-room was very pretty in a pink-and-white way, with a slender fairylike little body.

Laurie's work-mate was Fred, an old soldier of the First World War, a small spare man with a bushy moustache and twinkling eyes, and they were very attached to each other. Laurie took me home one week-end to stay with her sister's family, very kind friendly people. I was impressed with the way both parents, especially the father, handled the three small fair children; there was no slapping or crying in that house. We all went out to a park for the afternoon. One lunch-time I came upon Laurie outside the machinery depot practising hopscotch with fierce concentration. When I asked her what on earth she was doing, she said 'Remembering the game to teach my kids.' Sad to say, I heard later on that Ada and Margaret each had a miscarriage which was attributed to the strain of their work; I don't know about Laurie.

At Three Gates we had a gang of a dozen Italian prisoners of war, mostly foresters from the north, who had brown hair rather than black, and reddish-tan rather than olive skin. They wore dark brown battle-dress with coloured patches let into backs and knees, and khaki shirts. They were there to stook, cart sheaves, unload them and build the ricks and they worked like Trojans all day long, singing and cheerful, except for the tall, thin very dark corporal who was their foreman. He walked round languidly, looking as if work were beneath him, so I called him Adagio once or twice, which made him look down his nose still more. The girls didn't have anything to do but drive, but we were a bit short-handed once when there were two big four-wheeled trailers drawn up beside the ricks, so I couldn't resist saying 'Come on, I'll race you unloading these', just for the fun of seeing him work for a change. He looked even less pleased when I got mine done first and there were some amused grins among his mates. The happiest one rejoiced in the name of Ferruccio Spaggiari; one of my photos shows him riding on the load of sheaves smiling and waving an enamel mug. He and the others taught me a little Italian.

When any of us was starting to swing the starting-handle of her tractor, one of them would spring to do it for her, which is more

Joan, Margaret, Ferruccio and Ernie carrying wheat.

Dinner-time; Margaret, the cook and his mate.

than any of the Englishmen there or on any farm ever bothered to do, however ancient and liable to backfire the Fordson might be. They had a little curly-haired cook, a quiet young man whose duties were to brew up coffee, cook their midday meal and tidy up. When he saw the dry, curled-up sandwiches with little filling that we had in our lunch-tins, he looked horrified; from then on, every day he brought over to each of us a helping of the most delicious chips I have ever tasted, cooked in margarine, crisp and satisfying. He also gave us huge mugs of what I think was a mixture of coffee and cocoa; all this was nectar and ambrosia to us. On sweltering afternoons when we were grinding round hour after hour in roaring noise with the dust sticking to us, in uncovered tractors that were like ovens, he stood at the corner of the great field with a big shining tin of water and a mug and gave driver and binder-man each a drink every time we came round; it nearly fizzed on us! Every time I read the text about giving a cup of water, I think of him and the thoughtful way he and the others, officially our enemies, looked after us.

I was writing to my father about the different kinds of tractor we had in the depot, the Minneapolis Moline, known as Minnie, a great yellow creature with a high clearance – quite fun to get a lift on, roaring down the street – and the Caterpillar, also yellow, and the big red International, the last two track ones rather like tanks, for extra heavy work on very rough ground. I asked him to look out for tractors in the country at home and tell me what sort they were. 'If dark green, hefty and squat, they are Fordsons. If light grey with almost a car bonnet, they are probably Fergusons.' These were a pleasure to drive, for they had their own ploughs and other tools to hitch on that could be raised and lowered hydraulically, instead of the driver's having to lean back and yank on a rope to trip the plough out of the ground – and that didn't always work, so things could get very awkward as you came closer and closer to the hedge with the plough still stuck in the ground. Also, joy of joys, the clever little Ferguson had a self-starter; definitely one up for the Belfast engineer who designed her.

My father was helping to sort out my income tax. We were paid the princely sum of fifty shillings; it went up to fifty-two in the end.

Almost half of it went on board, insurance and tax; some of the excess tax they levied was eventually disgorged as post-war credits at about retiring age – fortunately index-linked. I was asking my mother to send on Readers' Union books and Horizon, and was delighted to hear that she had read with interest *The Story of a Norfolk Farm*, a key book, to me. I told them I'd heard from Mrs Devany in Easky, who had recovered from an illness and was out and about again, and asked that negatives of photographs should be sent to her. My Aunt Elsie had high blood pressure which was causing concern, and my mother was very busy with voluntary work,

'Giocoso'

housekeeping, and visiting her every day. I asked what they were doing about a holiday. One letter ends: 'Now I must go and scramble for a bath. One spends from morn to dewy eve getting dirty, and the evenings getting clean if one can! It never occurred to me before that hay and corn were such filthy stuff to handle. I'm getting quite a bit of fruit these days. I buy plums if we get off on Saturday by 5 or 6 o'clock, and we have them for dinner sometimes. Old Sid brings me a big juicy greengage every morning. He's a funny old devil, was a head farrier in the cavalry, is small and very square with ginger hair and a pair of arms like Popeye the Sailor's.' Diana was to take her finals next year and Maeve, my mother must have told me, was coming over to England to drive for the Red Cross. 'It would be too much to hope for her to be sent to the Birmingham area', I wrote. It was.

95

Peaceful Wartime

There was a dance at the hostel one evening. I was there, sitting in breeches and jersey like the others, wearing slippers I'd made out of buffalo hide. Suddenly one of the visiting soldiers asked me to dance, so I went and put on shoes, not wanting to contend with army boots. He was a very good dancer, but seemed a morose sort of chap.

After harvest we were all busy after the ploughmen, harrowing with an arrangement of three harrows, disc-harrowing with a frame containing two sets of discs at a slight angle to each other, working a cultivator like a harrow with each point turned forward and shod with a heavy arrow-head, or rolling. All this was to break up the ground, drag out any weed-roots, crush the clods and prepare a seed-bed for the next crop, probably winter wheat, to be drilled in. I was alone a lot of the time, buzzing up and down the field. If my tractor ever conked out I could usually get it going again by unscrewing the iron plate about six inches by four that served as a primitive carburettor, scraping the carbon out of the grooves with a screwdriver and fastening it on again. The engine was started on petrol; when it warmed up, you had to get off and turn the fuel switch from 'gas' (-oline) to 'T.V.C.' (tractor vaporising oil, alias paraffin). It didn't do to be absent-minded with petrol so precious that there were stickers on some tractors 'We won't waste it, sailor'; also, it was extremely awkward to run out of petrol miles from the depot. One day, sitting on the bank of a field eating my sandwiches, I realised that there was only one kind of dirt that mattered: just a smear of paraffin on your hands made the food taste horrible.

As autumn came on, it grew cold and comfortless in the hostel except round the stove in the dining-hall, and my upper bunk was too cold to sleep in, so I decided to look for a farm to move to. We went to Stoneleigh Abbey a couple of times, so I asked the agent, Major Lowsley-Williams if he needed a tractor-driver, he took me on and I got myself transferred.

Chapter Four

Stoneleigh Abbey

I WAS TO LIVE WITH Mr and Mrs Phillips, an elderly couple who
had a spare room in the cottage they rented on the estate over in
Ashow, the hamlet near which was the W.L.A. hostel where I had
been forewoman. Mr Phillips had worked on the Abbey farm until
he retired, and even at the age of seventy he was called upon to work
in busy times. He was small and thin with bushy white eyebrows and
moustache. Mrs Phillips was stout, energetic and outspoken. I doubt
if they had had much choice about having a land girl billetted on
them, but they put up with me with a good grace. I had a big bed
with a feather mattress which was very cosy, but I was not trusted to
make it; Mrs Phillips insisted on shaking it up properly for me every
day. I washed in cold water in my room in the morning and with a
kettleful of hot water in the scullery sink at night. I missed my bath,
but it was very nice to have my own quiet room, good home cooking
and my clothes washed for me.

There was no electricity or water laid on. Cooking was done on the
little range in the kitchen-cum-living-room, and sometimes Mrs Phillips put some big potatoes to bake in the oven all evening for supper.
After tea the table had its thick cover put on again, with the lamp in
the middle. They would read the paper or knit, and I got out my 'Teach
Yourself Italian', did exercises and learnt verbs till I nearly fell asleep.
I had to do something to keep my brains from addling altogether, once
I had come in, washed and oiled my boots with neat's-foot oil according
to Uncle Jack's instructions. I had soon discarded the W.L.A. boots
which were too pointed, and bought myself a pair of boy's boots; they
swore they could hear me coming clumping down the lane to the
cottage, with the boots leading the way and me following.

Stoneleigh Abbey

The estate was about two thousand acres, half of which was taken up by the deer park, where there was a big American military camp and hospital. I was amazed to hear from my mother that the Americans had also reached Warrenpoint. 'Fancy playing baseball in the streets! We hear great tales about the ones here. Some of the girls from the hostel who work here have the life teased out of them because they go out with the Yanks.' There were two other land girls living in lodgings and working on the farm, Phyllis, a very nice girl with a downright manner, great sense of humour and reddish-gold wavy hair, and Mary, big and gentle in movement, with a rather full, pale face.

The foreman, Fred Healey, and his brother Harry were second-generation Irishmen, but Harry was quite cross with me when I said something about it. I thought it was a pity to show himself ashamed of his ancestry, especially to me, as I was obviously neither a terrorist nor obliged to come over and join up. Their speech bore traces of Irish mixed with Warwickshire. George, with his black hair – what was left of it – and moustache and piratical black hat, was an old soldier in every sense, whose watchword was 'Keep gently going', though we used to say he spent a good part of the day lighting his everlasting pipe. Though I smoked an occasional cigarette, it came nowhere near a pipe as a time-waster; anyway I never wanted to smoke at work. I carried a tobacco-tin that held two or three cigarettes, matches and a needle for getting thistles out of my fingers or the men's; I couldn't bear to watch them hacking at their hands with a penknife, and got quite good at operating on other people.

There were two Italian prisoners who lived in a hut near the Abbey and had worked on the farm for a good while. Mario came from Perugia, had been a tank-driver in the army and was tall and very strong, with regular features, hazel eyes and wavy brown hair usually covered by a beret. If anything needed lifting or manhandling he was called into action and it was soon in order; no wonder he was rather conceited. His mate's name was, for a dark man, the unlikely Albino, but everybody called him Ben and he seemed quite content with it. He was smaller, with lashes long enough to keep out the dust, a big mouth and a very good tenor voice. Sometimes he used to stop in the middle of a field to deliver an operatic aria with great verve; 'Celeste Aïda' was his favourite, and he had been asked to sing 'Ave Maria' in church. For work he always wore a cloth cap back to front. The two seemed to get on all right usually but when Mario had, we thought, been throwing his weight about, Ben would be in a black mood and the gaiety of the work party was reduced till he recovered.

In mid-October they started lifting sugar-beet with three hostel girls helping. Whenever I had no tractor work I had a day at it too. They used a special small horse-plough to loosen the beet, which was big and heavy, about the size of mangels. Then pairs of us worked down the rows, pulled up two beet each, bashed them against each other to knock off the soil and threw them down in neat rows. The next two came along with heavy knives, lifted each beet by the root and sliced off the leaves. Afterwards the cart was taken down, the beet thrown in and the leaves raked up for cattle-feed.

Usually there were few at the job but today at last there was a determined drive with fourteen people, including the tractor men and others, who didn't do much but talk. Ben was fearfully energetic after sleeping all day on Sunday, he said, and fairly chuffed down the rows. As I was working opposite him, I also chuffed – phew! When I shut my eyes I see a huge beet with splayed leaves. Mario and I then ploughed them up and Mr Phillips finished it. It's the first time my back has really ached, potatoes or no potatoes, hoeing and weeding or no hoeing and weeding. Most of last week I was alone ploughing at Glasshouse all day; I wonder why a field here and there should be called that. I left my watch in Birmingham, so never even knew the time unless I called at the shepherd's house; one night I got back at six instead of five o'clock. Still, I'm not so punctual in the mornings. You should have seen it this morning at 7.15 – glorious bright moonlight! It looked extraordinary, and at 8.15 it was only just light enough to see what you were doing. It's the first time I've gone to work by moonlight at 7.45 a.m.

'I went to Leamington to see *The Petrified Forest* again, with Joan Hosker. I was a bit disappointed, and when we came out it was raining stair-rods to cycle back in. On Friday I went up to the hostel for an Ensa show, which wasn't much. I know more than half the girls there still.

'I've been thinking about getting home for Christmas, but only saw the Major on Saturday with Mrs Lowsley-Williams and a couple of kids, all on horseback, come down to see the beet. I said I was due for some leave and asked if they'd be giving a few days extra at Christmas as, I'd heard, they did last year, and he said I ought to get time for travelling. 'Yes,' said Mrs L. -W., who had just come back from her old home in Mallow, 'she'll need a day to get to Liverpool and another day to get home and two more to come back.' Good for her! But as Lady Leigh is on the W.L.A. committee, it wouldn't do for me to have too long. As a matter of fact, Phyl told me that now that I'm privately employed, the W.L.A. can 'go and scratch', so I'll see if I can get a passage and as long a time as possible. Yes, Lord Leigh is a Lt. Colonel, and they have several children. The eldest is John, a shy little boy of nine, very nice-looking, who came riding round with the Major one day and was introduced to me.

Part Two *Stoneleigh Abbey*

'The Italian is progressing slowly. I'm supposed to know it by Christmas, according to Mario, but I have grave doubts, especially if I have a lot more tractor work and overtime. I'm the only one who takes an interest in it; it would be a great waste of opportunity not to, as I have every intention of travelling some time. I won't be happy till I've seen oranges actually growing on a tree, and picked them. Uncle Jack says, from memories of his time in South Africa, that they taste quite different fresh. Ben says they have orange and lemon orchards in Sardinia. His English is very sketchy but he gives a graphic description of feast-days, dancing in the streets, fancy dress, masks and all, and harvest-home, with a dash of Venice with gondolas thrown in. Religion must be quite fun in a country like that, with all those saints' days. He's a sailor, and a carpenter in a factory at home. Mario is a tank-driver, so is very useful for starting up my old tractor when it's in a devilish mood.'

In fact, sometimes the starting-handle was impossible to turn, so I used to jump on it. If it had back-fired, I used to think I'd have been sent flying over the tree-tops. However, the poor thing was so cold from being left out in the frost under a lean-to shed that it probably hadn't the energy. Funny how the most decrepit and difficult-to-deal-with old wreck inevitably got left to the girl! 'Glad the bike is going strong, Pop. Don't know what I'd do without mine here. Be buried, I suppose.'

I had a great performance writing in good time to book a passage, applying to the Permit Office and filling in various forms, and at last managed to book by Heysham to Belfast. The trains were crammed, so I sat on my case in the corridor and read till there was room in a carriage. I wore uniform and found the forces very helpful. At Preston station some splendid women ran a free canteen for forces travelling; one of the soldiers brought me too a mug of tea and some sandwiches, to my surprise and gratitude. It did a lot for my hunger and even more for my morale to be included with them in such a kind and friendly way.

I felt I'd earned my leave. '*December 1st*: I can't remember when I wrote last. The weeks simply flash past. Last week we did four days' thrashing, awful in the Dutch barn and all right in the open, except that the wind blew back the chaff and cavings as I loaded the cart. I was part carter and took the loads away between times and emptied them by backing down a steep slope. Sez Fred: 'For God's sake don't go down that, now!' Later on Mr Phillips came and took over. He has been in bed with a flu cold since Monday and Mrs Phillips has caught it and been pretty bad, but crawling round and insisting on getting up at the usual time. All I could do was get in water and shoo her off to bed early. Most picturesque, pumping water by moonlight! The last rick we thrashed was linseed, alias flax. Seems a pity to waste all the straw. Linseed tastes quite like sunflower seed. I wouldn't mind eating linseed cake if I were a cow. I took a snap of the thrashing, though people were bustling about in front of one another.'

'Then we went lime-spreading. It was real pick-and-shovel work, as the bags of lime had been left out about two months and were frozen stiff anyway. We moved to a new field yesterday, just four of us, three from the hostel and myself. My hands are ingrained with lime and make a rasping noise when rubbed together. I need a bit more tractor work to grease them!

'Aunt Mary has flu, so I rang up last night and heard she was better. It's very funny when I ring up anyone; I have to go into the post office, which is in a front parlour with a little desk and a telephone near the door, and is inhabited by three old sisters and a brother who sit round solemnly doing their knitting and, I suppose, listening to my rather inane conversation.

'The other day, as we had been having a discussion on strength, Mario put me standing on a potato-fork and lifted me on it about nine inches in the air quite easily. I was impressed by this feat till yesterday when, one of the girls happening to have her foot on my shovel, I said for fun, 'O. K., get on it', and hoisted her up without killing myself. As she weighs 8 stone 4, the shovel about half a stone and I nine stone, I think it was quite a good effort! However I'm afraid I couldn't heave two hundredweight above my head as they say Mario can.'

The rest of the journey home for Christmas was rather weird. We

Stoneleigh Abbey Gatehouse

had to queue for well over an hour at the docks in darkness, edging forwards with our suitcases a foot or so at a time, everybody tired and silent, to get on board at last about one in the morning. As there were no berths to be had, I went to the dining-saloon to have a good supper and then parked myself and my luggage on the floor of the other saloon and tried to sleep. We tacked sharply – all ships did, of course, in case of U-boats – and as it was a stormy time of year, at a certain angle the waves suddenly began hitting the beam a tremendous wallop. I don't think I really worried about it, though.

Chapter Five

Thrashing

'25TH JANUARY, 1944. Last week we thrashed all the time. One place was out next the main road. The Americans used to come past with a queer little band of about a dozen black, white and yellowish men in overalls, stop opposite us and hang over the gate to watch. Sometimes a whole collection of them would come shuffling down the road, take a notion, break ranks and gape, much to our amusement. Three stray ones came along one afternoon when we were having a break, pressed two bags of 'candy' upon us and wanted to ride the major's horse. (So did we, for that matter.) I was on the wheat rick with Mr Phillips, who now gets roped in for thrashing too. Then I was helping to build the straw rick, a huge affair which ended most picturesquely with Ben pitching great heavy boltings of straw from the trusser at the back of the thrashing-drum up to Mary, ensconced in the pitch-hole in the side of the rick, who passed them up to me in another hole and so on to George who pranced about aloft like the fairy on the Christmas tree.

'Then we thrashed at the Abbey, where I got a photo from the straw-rick during a slight lull, of Ben pitching up the last few sheaves on to the drum, where Phyl was cutting bonds and Mario feeding the stuff into the drum. It's like a monster roaring 'More, more, more!' all day and breathing out clouds of filthy dusty rubbish at one side and, of course, streams of grain into the sacks at the back, which someone changes when they're full, and over-sized boltings of straw from high up at the back; they're too big because nobody can be bothered to adjust the trusser. I did chaff and cavings nearly all day because Lola, one of the hostel girls, was yapping about having to do it all. Must say I found it a soft job except for the dust, removing

Clearing-up.

Thrashing-gang Lunch.

the rubbish in sheets of sacking from time to time, instead of pitching those boltings above my head at full stretch. We had one afternoon riddling spuds for a change because of bad rain. One good thing is that we don't start till 8.30 or 8.50.

'On Saturday morning I turned wagoner and took the old mare and a wagon load of straw over to some cattle-yards. Mary and I were all morning clearing up that and the 'mullock' of weed-seed and stuff from under the drum, and she said, 'I wish we could get some folk out from a town to see what a damn job we have to do to get them their bit of bread!' It was 20 to 1 instead of 12 o'clock by the time I'd got a load of tackle to bring back for thrashing at the Grove on Monday, unhitched the mare and got her harness off in the stable; poor old girl, she thought she'd never get her dinner and I thought I'd miss my train to Birmingham, but I didn't. I was just dead – suppose it was the muggy weather. I was working all last week in overalls, minus jersey, with sleeves rolled up. I even cycled miles in that – in January!

'This week it's been really hectic. The Major took Phyl off to do ploughing or something without a word of warning, leaving us with only two on the straw rick. On Monday morning I did Bert Mills', formerly Ben's, job of lifting the straw from the trusser and pitching it up on to the rick. It came out so fast that I hardly had time to dash (perhaps dash is hardly the word for tacking against a strong wind with a damn great bolting on a fork above your head) there and back before another one came out – clickety-click. Mr Phillips

came in the afternoon. Then George pitched up to me and I caught and chucked to Mr Phillips who built the rick. The wind rose to a gale and we battled against it; the corner boltings were blown right up and off again and again, no matter what way they were placed. The major rode up, could see what a job we had and went away. We thought Phyl must be sick, as he didn't send her to help. It's amazing how quickly you recover; two or three times in the day you begin to feel you couldn't lift another bolting against the wind and yet, after a bit of a break, you can fling away. All the same, I was very concerned about old Mr Phillips having to work so hard up on top. I know his wife was pretty angry about it, though she didn't say much. In the evening I walked and ran a good way to the main road to go into Leamington to meet Laurie and Joan and go to a dancing-class, but as it was still wet and stormy they hadn't come, so I got the last bus back – at 8.30.

Ben.

'Yesterday we were building a second rick, throwing with the wind – what a difference it makes, when there's only one person to throw from one end of a twelve-yard rick to the other, or try. This afternoon we had a hostel girl to help, which made it much easier, though she didn't fancy the job much. I must say I rather enjoy thrashing. The whole gang is there and there is a great sense of urgency. Heavens, they are fairly slamming it through, too. We did a whole rick yesterday in spite of a couple of stops for rain. Mario and Ben are in great form again, Mario very affable and in a teaching mood again. I don't think there will be any more nonsense about 'weak land girls' and 'not being strong enough to go on the rick'!'

I was knitting a jumper for my mother and had written to Laura, Maeve and Honor, to the latter in an appalling mixture of three languages for her to decipher.

10th February: 'Have just had a bath at the hostel and could roll into bed any minute but must finish this, read a bit and do a spot of 'teaching myself' or evening will succeed evening and I'll have nothing done. There is such peace here compared with the hostel; I'd hate to live in one again. This afternoon during the break I was sitting on a rick-sheet on some sacks and couldn't think why it was moving about under me; got up, and so did a rather repressed-looking little mouse! Mary picked it up and we let it escape while the dog wasn't looking. He has caught plenty of huge fat rats, though. I hate them,

Bashing up lime to spread

"Tripping" the plough

but I'm afraid I'm still fond of mice; even if the rick is running with them I don't like killing them, except half-killed ones.

21st February: 'I have just bought myself two Christmas presents from you: two van Gogh prints, one of cornfields in Provence and one of a young man in a yellow jacket, both of which have been 'growing on me' for years. The rest of the money I'll spend on riding lessons if I can get any, when the evenings are lighter.

'We have done five weeks' thrashing straight off and still have about three weeks' to do. On Saturday Mr Phillips was told he needn't come, as one of the keepers was going to help. The morning wore on and he didn't come, so I took the straw boltings up from Ben and built the rick all on my own. Fortunately they came up only moderately fast, but though it was a frosty day with a cold wind, I certainly sweated – not that I got any credit for filling two men's places! This morning the boltings were still, according to George, about a quarter of a hundred-weight – well, slight exaggeration, but very heavy – so I struck and went on the corn rick for a change. Then in the afternoon Mary was away at the dentist's and Harry Healey wanted me to cut bonds, so I went up on the drum, passed each sheaf over to him as it came up and, armed with a large very sharp knife, cut the twine round each. I made one or two slight cuts along my fingers, which

Part Two *Thrashing*

poured blood. (What waste! It could have gone to the Eighth Army via the transfusion service.) Mario, who had taken over feeding the drum, got quite concerned and insisted on tying up my hand with my big hanky, rather to my amusement. I had quite a hectic afternoon, as I didn't want them saying I was slowing down the proceedings, not having done that job before. It's rather back-breaking, as you have to keep bending down and reaching over to the left to fish up the sheaves if the pitcher-up isn't an expert. Sorry if my writing's a bit erratic; I've spent over an hour this evening extracting tiny little thistles from all my fingers and if I'm not cross-eyed, I feel it!

'We see quite a lot of the Yanks these days, as we're working over near the Deer Park. Over the river they have various contraptions. Mary and I strolled up during our break to see the cables they had rigged up, one high for your hands and one lower for your feet, so of course I had to have a try at shuffling along them. I was most of the way across the river when I looked up and saw a horde of them descending on us, so retreated in good order. They came and did Tarzan stunts, swinging over the river on a rope hung from a tree top; some of them got splashed as they let their feet hang down too far. Much to our disappointment nobody fell into the water, though some made a good try! They also had a twelve-foot wall that they climbed up somehow at the back and dropped down at the front. One or two got stuck with their beam-ends in the air and had to go back the way they came. Then one funny little chap, all glasses and grin, came up and offered us gum, which we went back chewing.

'Some mornings Col. Upton takes Mr Phillips, George and me to work in the van, but George and I will be cycling in future, as Mr P. isn't coming. It takes about twenty minutes. The drive through the Abbey is so bumpy that my bike lamp fell off and the fastener-on piece broke off, but Mario soldered it during the week-end, having been a welder, and handy.

It felt very strange to have finished thrashing at last after seven and a half weeks. We felt almost bereft.

The 24th of March letter thanks my parents for sending sweets, a luxury, and goes on: 'I've been working overtime all this week except today sowing oats, barley or 'mixed corn' with Fred. He drives the tractor and I ride the drill to see that it's working properly all the time. All I need is a long tail to hang on with; it's a big modern drill meant to be worked from the tractor with ropes to put it in and out of gear with, so there's no board to stand on at the back. I sit on top of the seed-box and hope for the best, bumping over ridge-and-furrow fields. On Monday we went on till 6.45, on Tuesday till 7.45 (without a break from one o'clock) and on Wednesday till the same time, but with half an hour for tea, a great improvement. On Thursday Fred was going to a whist drive at the club, so then and today we stopped about 5.20, better and better.

'On Monday Phyl, Mary and I went to a party given by the Leamington Land Girls' Club, which we enjoyed. There was quite a nice crowd of girls, all from private farms. Phyl entered for the bun-eating contest; I held the string for her to bite the bun off and the prize was a dozen eggs, but we were beaten. I won third prize for guessing advertisements pasted up round the room and was amused to find myself the proud possessor of a set of packets of herb seeds, sage, fennel, sorrel and coriander – the sort of thing you come across in 16th century poetry – 'Coriander, sweet pomander.'

'Thanks very much for the shamrock. It came on the 16th, much to my delight, kept quite fresh in its native soil, and was duly worn. Part of it Mrs Phillips planted; she said there was lots of it in Gloucestershire where they used to live.

'Last week we spread some more lime. It is devilish hard on your hands and wrists and all your clothes feel horribly limy for days. It won't wash off your skin, of course, and putting on vaseline seems to make it stick worse. We also did some odd jobs of hay-carting, and George and I mixed fifty sacks of mixed corn – oats, barley, peas and beans to be sown for feed, while Fred fiddled about with the drill for two days. Dear me, such a palaver! You shoot it all out of different sacks, shovel it about in a huge heap on the concrete floor and spread tins of beastly-smelling yellow dressing powder on it which billows about and gets up your nose. Then you pour it bushel by bushel into big sacks again and move it to the side on a little truck. I find full sacks are not impossible to handle; I can lift about two hundred pounds off the ground and wallop it down to shake the stuff down without killing myself – at least I tried it once or twice just for curiosity. George shovelled and bushelled and I held the bags open and twiddled them away on the doodah. I'm thinking of going in for railway portering after the war!

'This week has been very cold work otherwise, perched on the drill. However, yesterday was mild and today not only spring-like but summery. In the evenings I'm still weaving up and down all the time as if I'd been on board ship. On Tuesday I had tea and supper in one at 8.15, washed and went straight to bed. Last night I went with Joan to the pictures in Leamington to see Walt Disney's 'Victory through Air Power', a quite good cartoon style description of the early planes, then diagrams of the Japanese and German 'zones' and how they should be squashed, the latter part being spoken by a U.S. aircraft designer, Selvez(?).'

Chapter Six

At Mrs Wilkinson's

A S MRS PHILLIPS had some relations who wanted to come and stay, or live there, away from their big town, it was arranged that I should move to Mrs Wilkinson's. She was a very nice woman who lived with her two small children in one of the four cottages called The Kennels, fairly near the Abbey and next to the road. 'It's rather awkward, as she has to change the rooms round and Mrs Phillips wants to spring-clean before her people come, so I told the Major he'd have to arrange for me to move in mid-week. Fred wants me for drilling till 4 tomorrow, Saturday, but I said I'd offered to give Mrs Wilkinson a hand, so they can fight it out, he and the Major. They have oil lamps there too, and no water laid on.' This letter was one of the few opened by the censor; I hope it made a little change for her!

'4th April. Well, they moved my luggage in the van on Saturday and I went off for the week-end. Mrs Wilkinson actually likes the idea of having a lodger as her husband is in the Merchant Navy and there are just the two kids and herself. Robert is nearly four and Chris is ten months, a good-humoured kid, but how I wish he could have a silencer fitted (he does train-whistle shrieks of energy); however, so does his mother. My room is small but nice, with pale green walls and plenty of room to put things. I go through their room to get to it, and the stairs lead down, boxed in, with a latched door at the bottom like the Phillips' to the sitting-room, big and comfortable but rather dark because of the trees. There is a tiny kitchen just big enough to eat in, and a scullery the same size, and then you're outside.

'Mrs Wilkinson was a stewardess on the Orient Line before the war, and made three trips to Australia. I tried to persuade her not to

Mrs Wilkinson with Robert and Chris, aged four and one.

bring me a cup of tea when she
calls me, but she swears she always makes it for herself first
thing, so I have it, though I feel
most luxurious and un-Land-
Army-ish.

Chris.

'The last two weeks have
been mostly drilling corn, and
there are still two days to do
when it clears up. It's been wet
since Sunday, deep puddles all
down the drive and lashings of
red mud where the timber-wag-
ons charge up and down. On
Friday Ben and Mario, Phyl and
I loaded thrashing-rubbish and
straw from near the drive and
took them over to some cattle-
yards; then loaded bales of straw and took them to other cattle
buildings. We had a good way to go with each load, down the drive,
round a field beside the river and over a lot of bumpy ground, saying
'Well, if it falls off, it falls off and that's that'. Then the way led
through a field full of rough black cattle that gazed solemnly at us
all the time and gathered at the gate to watch the proceedings. It
was a queer day, bitterly cold one minute and warm the next. We
got a good laugh out of everything that happened.

'As for Saturday, well, nobody remembered that it was April Fools'
Day but nothing could go right all the same. First Fred's tractor conked
out, which is most unusual. Then Mario pumped up the wagon tyre,
which waited till his back was turned and then exploded triumphantly.
The local garage had mended (sic) a puncture in it three weeks ago
and, as Fred remarked 'That tyre was about to lay an egg ever since'.
So Fred sent me to look for Harry, who was working in the Deer
Park, to tell him we couldn't come drilling. Off I went on my bike
and rode up hill, down dale and round trees till I found him. I didn't
get run over by a jeep or an armoured car, though the latter have

great races up and down the most impossible tracks, up gradients of one in two or so; they have a big stamping-ground in the middle, a huge bare patch.

'On returning, I was unfortunately collared by the Major, while the rest of the gang, Phyl, Ben and Mario, went off to load hay. He sent me with the shepherd to bring in a heifer and calf from the far end of the estate. Off we set gaily enough in the float drawn by a wayward old cob. When we were nearly there, we discovered he had the bit under his chin, so this was hastily remedied. Then we had to get the white calf up into the float with a struggle, as it suddenly developed appalling energy and obstinacy for a thing born the day before. Talk about noise! The cow trotted behind, stopping at more and more frequent intervals to graze, apparently forgetting her off-spring and then coming on again with reproachful mooings. Eventually we got to the cow-yard at the Abbey.

'The next job was to get a load of kale for the dairy cows, but first I had to take some churns to Bill the cowman, who was playing with his new milking-machine in the field. It's like an outsize caravan. The sides lift up, the cows walk in at one side, are milked and walk out at the other side. As soon as Bill got the churns off, the shaft broke. He pushed the harness one way and another and told me to take Bob back, plus float, but I wasn't having any of that, as Bob was looking funny. Sure enough, when Bill took hold of the bridle, off he went and careered round the field in small circles with Bill hanging on grimly. I can tell you I got out of the way in double-quick time. What with this wild horse, a bull in the field and some of the cows being chased by the dog, I felt it was no place for me! However, when they came back from their trip, I got Bob across to the farm without incident, and the shepherd and I fetched the load of kale.

'Mary is helping with the cows now and does nearly all the work while Bill plays about with the milking-bail. She is supposed to muck out the calf-pens in her spare time but never has any, and is now on holiday. Bill never cleans out if others can be roped in to help, so blow me if Phyl, Ben and Mario weren't busy with forks and much swearing when we got back. However, luckily it was twelve o'clock before anything else could go wrong.

Water supply round in the wood (pump for 4 cottages).

The Kennels, four cottages.

Peaceful Wartime

'Yesterday it poured, so we did odd jobs. Phyl and I tied up masses of thatching-pegs or 'sprays' in the morning. In the afternoon I straightened used baling-wires with Mario and discussed racing-cars. Incidentally, I told him about our O. M., which he says stands for Oficina Mecanica, a firm that makes mostly big lorries and such, road-signs and weights and measures, even our wonderfully compli-cated English variety! Today Phyl and I put through the mill about thirty hundred-weight of oats and beans and shovelled them into sacks, weighed them and carted them away on the little truck. There was plenty of flour flying about and we were well powdered, eyelashes and all. However, it's better than dust. I got my fill of that last week, a bad throat and a sticky cough. The dust even stopped my watch.'

Talking of dust, water was even more of a problem at the Kennels. To draw it, we had to take a couple of buckets round two other cottages into a little wood to get to the pump. I have a photo of Robert, aged four, manfully swinging on the handle, watched by Chris. Again we had earth-closets; even Stoneleigh village was without drains for many years after that. One result of this primitive state was that I was allowed to go up to the Abbey once a week for a bath, to my great joy. The bathroom I used was in the oldest part of the house, built of sandstone blocks. Armed with my towel and sponge-bag, I went down a long stone-floored passage to what I called my tenth-century bathroom, quite a large one.

'Lately we've been doing yet more lime-spreading. After using slaked lime before, we now used the burning kind, and had some windy days that did our eyes no good. Yesterday we – mostly Phyl and I – had a row with Mario. She was bringing up the empty trailer to load from the pile of bags. There wasn't much room, and he began waving her first one way, then the other. Neither of us knew what he meant and, as she made to get off and look, he bawled at her 'Come on!' and went on shouting. We both turned and told him he wasn't foreman, so he got very annoyed and said he wouldn't come back after dinner. We were working in two teams, two people loading a wagon and two spreading lime from another as it was driven along. Mario sulked all morning, went home early and came back still cranky after complaining to Fred. I had the argument out with him again as patiently as possible – it all seemed such a fuss about nothing, as Phyl always tries to place wagons conveniently for loading. Then we wrangled it out again, as we object to tale-telling. Fred just let Mario change his job, without telling us anything. In fact Fred seemed to expect Phyl to say something. He was very pleasant to her this morning but she told us she was so fed up that she took no notice. We were getting on fine before, and getting rid of the lime in style, so we were very disgusted at all this.

'Today Phyl, Mary, Ben and I took a horse and cart and went over to the Deer Park to fork up squitch, scutch, twitch or couch off the top of the ground where it had been harrowed and left in untidy piles here and there. The harrower should have done it, but it's a slow job while the tractor's waiting. We were then to cart it off.

'It was a glorious day and peaceful until Babs, the mare, started walking about on her own. She just would not stand still; we were hoarse shouting 'Woa!' or 'Wo-wa!' which seemed to have a little more effect, and tired running to grab her. I think she has a mouth of brass. Ben was very fed up but we three thought it was better to laugh than cry. At 4.30 we emptied the cart of squitch for the last time and brought her up to where we'd left our bikes. Mary held her head while we put the bikes and Babs's dinner-basin into the cart and Phyl and I got in among them. Babs got away somehow and off we went, with Phyl trying to stop her, but she hadn't got hold of the reins properly, so Babs was by then going at a good trot right under the trees, with us shouting 'Woa!' and ducking for our lives. Phyl got worried and we two made for the back of the cart. I fell out somehow and tore after the damn thing now heading for a steep hill down the field, while Mary and Ben just stood sort of mesmerised. Strangely enough, I got to Babs's head and hung on to the bridle till she stopped and we both breathed heavily and I tried to laugh at the same time.

'Then we all got into the cart and Ben, crouched on his knees in front, gripped the reins while Phyl and I clutched each other and bits of bicycle at the back. We went out on to the road, having decided it was safer than bumping over hill, dale and rut over the park. Babs trotted furiously down the hill, breaking into a canter or a gallop towards the bottom, in spite of Ben's pulling back for all he was worth. However, the rest of the journey was comparatively safe and peaceful, though she insists on charging even uphill at a great rate. We finally reached the Abbey at 5.10, to find poor Harry Carter waiting since dear knows when to take her in. He's Mrs Wilkinson's brother. He came to tea later on and I gave him all the grisly details, which seemed to amuse him very much. It's funny, that was the other thing I had in the back of my mind that I'd like to say I'd done, besides charioteering along in my cart as at Idlicote: stop a runaway horse. Join the Land Army and see life!

'Train back from Oxford, Sunday 4th June. I was delighted to hear that Brian dropped in and is in his old form; it seems years since we heard anything of him. What did he think of my present occupation, if anything? It was a year on the first of June since I began work.

'Summer having come again, I was bitten by the travel bug. I nearly went cycling last week-end, but better judgement and weariness prevailed and I just cycled to Birmingham (about 17 miles) and had a pleasant, restful time. This time I went to Oxford on a long-promised pilgrimage. Oxford is crowded; I knew that, but not how crowded. I tramped round and tried about six places before being told to 'Try the lady over there', who looked resigned and amused and said 'All right, I can do it; come along', and parked me on a divan in one of the sitting-rooms, a very nice room looking on to the garden. She left me to play with the radio, a rare treat, and dished up a wizard supper of bacon and egg, sausage and fried bread, cheese and salad. I heard a B.B.C. concert, wrote to Honor, finished my book and talked to a very obvious student who breezed in and out, said he came from Devonshire and proceeded to eulogise its cream with gusto. The next morning he appeared in a scarlet dressing-gown for breakfast, which was already an interesting meal because of the couple I was talking to about land work. They had asked if it was really as romantic as it sounded, and were very amused to hear the low-down. Willie, the student, then gave a hilarious description of his efforts to learn to ride for ten days, starting by cantering; apparently as the horse's back came up, Willie was just coming down and altogether it was a smashing success.

'Well, off I set, bright and early (after 11) to follow the itinerary given to me by a little tobacconist opposite Christ Church whom I'd asked if there were any guide-books to the city. I walked round Christ Church, along the path through the meadows to the Cherwell, where there are all sorts of boats and boat-houses belonging to the colleges, and along the river to Magdalen. I looked in at Queen's, Trinity, All Souls', Wadham, Lincoln, New College, Worcester and Keble, which differs from all the others in being of red brick with criss-cross patterns. I let myself in at the west door of the chapel, sat down in a seat near the door, to rest my feet, and found a Bible containing the Apocrypha. I would have loved to stand up and read aloud the story of Bel and the Dragon, concerning Daniel, as the acoustics should be good. Very few of the colleges are open on Sundays, but I think most of the porters would have let me in, as I could only come then. The few I spoke to were very decent, especially the one at St John's, of whom I enquired whether they kept track of their old students, in particular Jeffery, C. G., that is, Charlie. Oh yes, he remembered him well, got out the records, and there he was as large as life, as Sub. -Lt., R.N.V.R. He said that was well out of date and he might be anything by now. I was delighted to hear that he and presumably his family (from the address) are going strong. 'He was a rowing man', said the porter, so I couldn't resist telling him we learnt to row in the same boat. Of course after all this, he pretty well conferred on me the freedom of the college, gardens and all; anyway, I'd said I was a graduate of Trinity, Dublin.

'More and more, as time goes on, I'm glad of that. I'd never have known half what I'd missed if I hadn't gone to College, but I'd have missed such a lot. I don't even feel an outsider wandering round some strange college. What I'm trying to say is that, taken all in all, the effort of Mod. most definitely included, it was the best thing I ever did, and no matter what I did or am doing afterwards, (inappropriate as it may seem to you at present) it's something solid behind me that gives me confidence when talking to educated people and is no stumbling-block in the way of getting on with farm folk who, after all, are educated in things we are only learning.

'I've been so thrilled all day that I thought I'd better write at once. Colleges and students make me homesick in a way. Though I missed Trinity's 18th-century-rebuilt cleanness of line and spaciousness, I loved the Oxford colleges I've seen so far. They are mostly yellowish-grey stone, weathered and flaked in places, full of Tudor windows, fancy roof-edgings and carving, beautifully ancient, some with cloisters, and all built round quadrangles with lovely lawns.

'Oh, and who should I sit down beside in a café but Elizabeth Nesbitt, who was at school and college with me! I didn't like her much when we were kids, but we were very pleased to see each other. To crown it all, we had an Irish waitress who asked if I'd like 'something with a knife and fork to it': a grand week-end!'

That was another letter for the censor, and I wouldn't have swapped jobs with her. I hope it gave her a bit of amusement.

Chapter Seven

Haymaking and Harvest

'19TH JUNE. Thank you both for your letters. Pop, you make me envious with your description of the baths. We could just do with them on the farm! I would have written before, only that our own private and particular 'Second Front' started on Tuesday, and we worked till 8.30, 7.30, 8.30, and will do the same tomorrow. I trust we'll have Saturday afternoon off as Fred intends to, as I hope to go to Stratford with Joan and Laurie for the week-end.

'Fred, Phyl, Mary and I are working the hay-baler. We finished one big field, 'Anne's Close', last night and are in a huge one now of twenty-one acres, 'Cow Pasture', beside the drive and the Kennels, which is handy. It's not really a hard job, threading wires, but it's very trying when they aren't straight and won't go through, and jumping down off our board seats to up-end the bales – some weighing over a hundredweight – when they work their way through, and take up the board to Fred is warm work in the blazing sun we're having now – real haymaking weather. The tractor and baler go down the rows at a slow walking pace, picking up the hay. I have a photo of us baling straw during thrashing; in it I'm actually wearing breeches instead of dungarees, as it was very cold and I didn't need to bend my knees at that job. The last lot was quite good; they did me two postcards of each, so I was able to give Ben some that he was in, as I'd promised, and he was pleased.

'The others are picking up the hay with tractor, four-wheeled trailer (wagon) and hay-loader behind. Albert the cowman is making a neat job of rick-building. They rope in the shepherd too, sometimes, to drive. Phoebe is working with Albert; she came down to us at 8.30 looking as clean as a new pin, wearing a white hat and shirt. We were

'There goes a good clump!' George, Phyl and Ben unloading manure.

full of dust and hayseed – I was like a coalman! Naturally, the hotter the day, the more it sticks, and wearing goggles is nearly as bad as having the stuff blowing in your eyes all the time. We have to keep on our overalls or get covered with oil and dust inside as well.

'Friday. Nice and cool today – great difference. Before and after tea we loaded bales, using an iron handle with a big hook, which you wallop into the far side of the bale and use it and your knee to shift the thing. The men picked them up on to the wagon and I loaded with Mary or Ben. At dinner-time Lady Leigh, Col. Upton, the Major and a friend of his all came and took over our job. They sure made some funny bales: some miserable little things and some great coffins. We saw them at it when we came back, Lady Leigh doing my job, looking as if she was enjoying it, and the Major doing Mary's. Fred said tonight 'Ah, I told them the girls had a good laugh; they thought they couldn't do baling before but they know they can now!' As it isn't often he sticks up for us a bit, I was wondering what was coming

Phyl and Ellis wiring, Fred on the baler.

next. They made an elegant pyramid of bales, on which I photographed my four mates later on.

'Last Saturday I cycled five miles to Coventry to see the Sadler's Wells Opera Company in *The Bartered Bride*. Then I decided to stay for the evening show, as I really wanted to see *The Marriage of Figaro*, so I rang up Aunt Mary, had tea and went. It was worth it, though I was very tired by the end. Then I cycled to Birmingham, stopping for a drink on the way as I had a fierce thirst and saw a pub that looked quiet and not strewn with Yanks. It seemed to put great energy into my legs, as I fairly shot up the hills and got there in an hour and a half.

'Phyl, Mary and I had managed to fit in three riding lessons at Miss Hollick's riding stables nearby, on lovely horses with perfect manners. My first was an elderly Irish hunter that felt like an armchair. We did various exercises, lying back, leaning to right or left, riding without stirrups at a walk and so on, and got on with trotting quite

Ben, Phyl, Mario and Mary.

well. Then I was given a livelier young chestnut and we got on faster. My horse broke merrily into a canter the last time as I was going down the field by myself. She said I was making him trot too fast – it isn't a common failing of his – in fact she said I was going hell-for-leather, which really made my day!'

Alas, we never had time during the summer to arrange for any more lessons. However, I have a delightful memory of that ride.

'The five of us have been hoeing at odd times. While Fred and Mario were moving the baler and taking off part of it to fit it through the gate, Ben and I went over to Bachells to hoe one morning, and Mary and I finished it today. About six Americans appeared there, supposed to be running, with their P. T. instructor. One came along with some cigarettes and one of the others shouted 'Look out, he's a Wop!' One of them wouldn't believe me when I said 'These are swedes, not weeds.' 'Quit kiddin',' says he. 'They're cabbages!' It was after ten by then and, as Mary said, we had a fresh job, which expression amused them highly. We retired in good order and did them out of the pleasure of watching us work.

'On June the 21st I was to go to Stratford with Laurie, but as she couldn't get away I went by myself. I had a job finding anywhere to stay; however at last I was directed to a very nice private house where they fit in a couple of people if they like the look of them, more or less. It was like the time I went to Oxford. The owner asked if I'd mind sleeping on a divan bed in the sitting room, so I said I wouldn't mind the floor itself if she didn't mind its being slept on, and I was very comfortable. I had really meant to go to the Memorial Theatre, so I went, late as it was, and stood and then sat on the gangway, to see *Richard II*. It was pretty good, especially Richard, who had a fine voice reminiscent of MacLiammóir's.

'On Sunday I went for a row on the river, as I hadn't been in a boat for ages (not since Christmas; that was lovely!). I had a good lunch in the town and went out to investigate Anne Hathaway's cottage, which was really worth seeing, though I had expected to be disappointed. The Hathaway family lived in it till 19-something and all the furniture is theirs, or was, and is ancient and genuine, so they swear. There were swarms of Yanks, hikers and bikers.

George and Mary, loading sheaves.

Fred Healey and Bunny cutting Wheat.

Part Two *Haymaking and Harvest*

'We've had a queer lot of jobs lately. It was too wet most of last week to make hay. The five of us mugs went thistle-cutting in a small patch of flax, which they call linseed here, and had to spend half the time sheltering under the trees as it absolutely poured. The next game was singling the sugar-beet which was done quickly by four very casual labourers, Irishmen, I regret to say. The Major had looked at it and paid them and, as he didn't know a good job from a bad, they gave him a bad one. As the plants were by then too big to be done with a hoe, we did them by hand. It was hard on your head bending nearly double all day, and made the backs of your legs ache. However, it poured yesterday, Monday, so we had a change.

'We went up to the granary and straightened used baling-wires. Then we did a great spring-clean of the adjoining loft, moving a lot of junk: cooking gear that had belonged to the Gloucester Hussars. The things were let down out of one door on a rope by the Major and me, carried across by Ben, and the rope was then thrown up to Mario, who hauled them up to a store on the other side of the yard entrance and with Mary, packed them into place. There was a pile about four feet high of pie-dishes, which were let down in fours, but most things had handles. The worst thing was a big heavy machine like a mangle, but luckily it didn't have to go up. Another awkward object was a heavy wooden telephone box in six pieces. Ben caught each, acted as a human crane and swung it round to Mario. Then we swept and garnished the place ready for harvest. We were thinking of celebrating by having a dance up there!

'Today we thrashed most of an oat rick that has been lying in wait for us all this time. Luckily it wasn't very hot, but there was a horrible amount of rubbish.

'At the house we've had an 'Invasion' from London. Mrs Blizzard and three young Blizzards, one in the W.A.A.F.s and two younger ones, a very nice family.

'Could you please send my John Donne?

'18th July, 1944. The weather's still queer – hot and thundery, then cool, then stuffy again. Fred had to plough in 35 acres of hay that the major had insisted on having cut and which got left in the rain too long. There must have been nearly a hundred acres of hay altogether and we still have to bale or carry 37 acres; it will be harvest time before we're finished. Lately we've had various jobs such as singling beet and hoeing bracken among the potatoes in the Deer Park. We planted them with dried sewage, by the way. (They eventually made a very good crop.) Joan has just been out from the tractor depot ridging them up.

'On Friday Mr Wilkinson turned up for the week-end, his first leave since February. He brought masses of food, chocolate, clothes for Robert and stockings for Mrs Wilkinson, a box of oranges, cigarettes and a bottle of navy rum which was left for us to finish. I much prefer it to whisky – why didn't I join the Wrens! The house looked like Christmas Day pre-war, with things from all over the world: Australia, South Africa and U.S.A.

'Otherwise nothing much has happened lately, except that Ben went down with tonsillitis on Thursday week after going to the pictures at the P. O. W. camp and tearing back by bicycle in the cold. They moved him to Warwick Hospital, so on my way to Birmingham by bike I called in with some eggs Mrs Phillips gave me for him and an orange from Mrs Wilkinson, meaning to leave them and go on. However, I had such a job finding the right landing to leave them that when they asked if I'd like to go in, I thought I'd better, though I felt a bit daft walking down a great long ward clutching the parcel. Still, he looked in need of cheering up, propped up on a board like a photo frame, so I was glad I'd gone. There were a lot of Irish nurses there; I was talking to one from Cork. Phyl, Mary and I meant to go over on Thursday, and to go to the pictures in Leamington afterwards, but of course the weather turned hot, the hay was ready and though we did the baling we set out to do in good time, we only had to go on and bale another part after tea till nine o'clock. That always seems to happen when you plan to do anything.

'This double summer time is simply maddening. We start at 7.30 when it's not 5.30 by the sun, so the dew is on the hay or corn till about nine, or even 10.30 if the morning is dull. Then we have to go on working at night to make hay, having filled up the morning hoeing weeds: docks, 'muckle-weed' and old George's favourite, spotted

Ellis shucking wheat.

persicaria; it has smooth, pointed, very green leaves with a dark patch on each, and little pale pink beady flowers.'

I was very impressed with George's erudition, and am delighted to find the plant in Keble Martin's book, and to discover that it is, as suddenly occurred to me, a near relation to the 'hindering knot-grass' to which Helena compared Hermia in *A Midsummer Night's Dream*.

There is a most tantalising reference to some disaster about which, perhaps, on account of the censorship, I could not be explicit:

'My goodness, what a lot of excitement! It does seem awful for men to be wasted in an accident like that, rather in the way that it happened near here one day' – that was when we saw a small plane going downwards in the distance and heard it had crashed in a field. 'I didn't see anything about it here, of course. Northern Ireland might be blown up and the *Daily Sketch* wouldn't turn a hair, and our wireless is still conked. How lucky you didn't get hit by anything, Dad. I simply can't imagine such a catastrophe happening in such a frightfully ordinary place, but there you are.

'I have decided to buy records because I get no music nowadays except a bit on the wireless at week-ends. I ordered three in Dale Forty's in Leamington and have collected two: one is Jean Sablon singing modern versions of 'Sur le Pont d'Avignon' and other songs rather like 'Boum' that I have at home; the other is one Lindsay had at school, that I loved, Hugo Wolf's 'Italian Serenade'. Little Robert likes the Avignon one and sings 'Telephone, telephone' after it!

'*3rd August*. Stoneleigh Fête was on Saturday and we went with two ponies from the Abbey to give rides to kids. We listened to Lady Leigh introducing the Mayor and did a tour round. Mary waited ages in a queue to have her fortune told but I got fed up and went and won a pound of tomatoes by throwing three darts at a board whizzing round; needless to say, I would hardly have made fifty if it had been standing still! Then I didn't do much except collect Phyl's threepences for rides, which amounted to 19/6, so I might as well have gone to Aunt Mary's at the usual time instead of arriving at 11 o'clock at night.

'They had my old tractor mended – new ball-race in the front wheel – so I've been using it last week and this. I hadn't realised how much I'd missed having one, though it's often good crack working with the gang. It still uses several quarts of oil a day instead of a week; I can't think why they didn't have it re-bored all the time it was standing idle. The radiator leaks, but that's nothing – so does Phyl's. It means carting about an extra bucket or more of water. It used to annoy me when people said 'It must be a nice job; you just sit on the tractor.' They don't know how much messing about there is in tractor-driving. First you fill up with petrol, paraffin (not from a pump but from tins you hoist up), water – two or three bucketfuls, including some for the air filter, which in modern tractors is an oil one – engine oil, gear oil occasionally and grease up and then swing it. During this process, Phyl and I grin at each other and say 'You see, you just sit on the tractor!' Still it's well worth it when you get started. You can see what you're doing and what you've done, changing the whole look of a field in a day.

'At present we're doing all the ex-hayfields. Harry Healey and Phyl were ploughing while I followed with the drags, heavy harrows slung three on a beam which you hit while turning if you're not careful, to break the furrows down smooth. Now Phyl's dragging one field while I'm scuffling the first one; that is, using the cultivator. After dragging it four times and cultivating it down, I'm beginning to know it! It's getting like a very choppy sea, all big lumps of squitch rearing on end. It's almost like ploughing, as I have to do it fairly deep.

'They started cutting oats on Tuesday; I've seen two fields cut and shucked (stooked) this week. I went to the pictures last night with Joan, who says they're going out to Three Gates today cutting. I said I wished I could go with them; somehow we all got an affection for Three Gates, where we worked last year for five weeks or so cutting and carrying, War Ag, Land Army, ten Italians, Uncle Tom Cobbley and all – oh, those chips and coffee!

'Ben came back on Friday after eighteen days away. Mrs Fern, who lives over the arch into the stable yard, stuck her head out as Phyl and I went to work, and asked if we had any news of him. When I came back at dinner-time she called again, and up there he was. He said he had a rotten time in Warwick Hospital; the doctor looked at him about once, ordered him some pills and took no more notice.

Peaceful Wartime

The nurses were all right but the food was rotten. Fancy giving anybody with tonsillitis bread and cheese and other dry things to eat! They sent him to camp after five days and then he went to the military hospital a few days later, still bad, and was much better treated for the next week. He ended up playing billiards and darts with the soldiers and peeled spuds for something to do.

'We have the equivalent of an evacuee here at the moment. His mother is expecting another baby, and Mrs Wilkinson, being very kind-hearted, rashly took on this kid of a year and eight months, a miserable little devil, always screaming, and no wonder. Apparently at home he is locked in a room with nothing but his bed in it and left to screech while they go out in the evening, and so on. He has improved very greatly and is almost house-trained and human now, though he still doesn't talk, but usually looks happy now for a change. There are quite a lot of evacuees round here, two next door, mother and baby.

'If you can get hold of South Riding by Winifred Holtby, read it; it's very good indeed.

'22nd August. I was delighted to hear that Miss Patton came to see you. Often and often I wondered what had become of her in the last twelve months. I didn't like to bother her by writing, and I thought if she had time to write she'd have written to my home address. I can't say how pleased I am that you have met each other.'

They had shown her a recent letter from me, and she wrote and said I should write about my Land Army experiences and call the account 'The Good Brown Earth'. I would have liked to, but didn't get round to it, and anyway other people were getting their books about the land published soon after the war, and I felt forestalled.

'Last night Joan and I met in Leamington to eat and go to the concert by the Hallé Orchestra, but when we'd been there fifteen minutes they informed us that it was off because the railway had made a mistake and sent the instruments to Bath! Joan went home today, so I went by myself. Albert Coates, the conductor, is rather fat but none the less energetic and quick. It was pretty good, but one's attention was apt to be a bit distracted by the cold, as the concert was in a glass pavilion in Jephson Gardens, and we are suffering a cold snap. I wore my uniform, the first time for months. The thing I liked best was Debussy's *L'Après-midi d'un Faune*, which had grown on me of late years. They finished with a very noisy Tchaikovsky symphony, No. 4, with a lovely pizzicato movement in the middle that runs on and on. They also played a Haydn (London) one that I found I knew. I shall never know the names of things if I live to be a hundred and one. I was so cold that I didn't get to sleep till 12.30 the last couple of nights. Don't think I haven't enough blankets. I much prefer this to the heat-wave we had before, when I couldn't sleep for the heat. Nothing like contrast!

'This is a messy sort of harvest. We haven't done any of it this week because of heavy rain since Saturday when I was driving my tractor for the carrying gang. We built a huge rick of good wheat and, about nine o'clock, fetched a load of straw to top it up with, and then they havered about and left it till morning. About seven a.m. it lashed down rain! The thing is, the Major expects the weather to last until he's finished. He never even got an extra hand, except two elderly chaps on the estate, and refused the offer of the two men who fiddle about with the milking-machine and do less than anyone else. Fred, Harry, Phyl and I were ploughing and cleaning the fields that were fallowed for winter oats, in the meantime. I worked till 8 o'clock last night and 7.15 tonight, when it rained and the ground got too heavy and 'reaved up' in the drags, so I packed it in and went home. This fallowing is a good idea; it's a pity one couldn't do it for the garden. If the ground is ploughed in summer and the weeds are left to sprout, they can be rooted out each time till the supply is more or less exhausted. I shall be disgusted if my field grows weedy corn, as it will have been done over seven times when I've finished.

'I spent some time this morning decarbonising. That sounds better than saying I unscrewed the manifold, or what passes for a carburettor, and scraped or chiselled off quantities of black, rock-like stuff. It hadn't been done for about two years; beats me how the old thing goes so well. I just struck at driving it like that, and demanded spanners to take over to the Grove, as Fred was beginning to say 'I'll take that plate off some wet day', and I thought 'Yes, you'll go fooling round with my tractor and I'll go grinding cattle-feed in the mill-house and get all full of flour.' I like to do things myself; then I know whether they're done or not. Glover's of Warwick are supposed to have overhauled the tractor a good while ago. Perhaps they did only the wheel that was coming off!'

Modernity was raising its head, and a combine harvester had appeared on the scene, such a thing as Uncle Jack told me had been used in Australia donkeys' years ago.

'Harry was driving the combine while we, Fred and co., were carrying. It 'beats as it sweeps as it cleans', or rather thrashes as it cuts. The two Italians and Tom Soulby were lugging the sacks about and Phyl was driving wagons for them. They were doing about nineteen tons a day, and the grain merchants took it straight away. When we were thrashing, we did about fifty-four sacks a day – that is five tons eight hundredweight – and that was the work of ten or eleven people instead of five!'

Tom was a pleasant young man, a friend of the Major's, I think, who had come to spend some time doing various jobs to learn practical farming. He came along wearing a sports coat, flannels and a hat when he first joined us for hoeing, which caused us some amusement.

Of course the combine, an exciting, roaring great creature itself, took the drama out of harvesting in a way – and the uncertainty – and it was good to see such a lot of hard work saved. When we looked back to the first part of this year's harvest and seven weeks' thrashing in the new year, we reckoned that each sheaf was moved eight times from cutting and binding to shucking (or stooking), carrying, unloading, rick-building; then for thrashing, rick-unbuilding and handling several times.

As autumn drew on, we were all busy ploughing stubble and cultivating, then drilling winter wheat and some oats, with artificial fertiliser trickling through the drill at the same time as the seed corn. Once the sugar-beet and this year's potatoes had been lifted, the latter picked up by local children, we loaded trailers with manure from farmyards about the estate to put on various potato-fields for the next year's crop.

When we were cleaning up at the Grove, Mario, being the tallest, used to pick us all some apples from a couple of old trees there; they had a delicious old-fashioned flavour. At least, driving a trailer-load of muck was easier than getting through fairly narrow gateways with a load of sheaves. No matter what we said, the men would always load the big four-wheeled trailers as wide as possible and stand back watching us manoeuvring them delicately through. We never gave them the satisfaction of getting stuck, even with one old devil of a trailer that had a habit of swinging slightly from side to side so that we had to allow for that. We also got used to having to back the tractors with trailer hitched on, including this 'okkard' old one.

Another autumn crop I discovered unexpectedly was enormous mushrooms. George assured me that they could be eaten, though he called them horse-mushrooms, so I took a couple back to Mrs Wilkinson, who had to cook them one at a time, as each was nearly the size of the frying-pan. I was very hungry and they were delicious.

As the mornings grew darker, for some time we used to meet at eight o'clock in the old harness-room at the Grove. It was too dark for a photo, alas, but I have a vivid picture in my mind of Harry and George, Ben and Mario, Mary and Phyl leaning against the walls and the old bits of harness, having a smoke or a chat by the warm yellow light of a hurricane lamp, waiting for it to get light enough to work on a dark cloudy morning, or for the rain to stop. The setting had almost the air of a Nativity scene.

I had the same job as last year of catching the Major at the right moment to fix my Christmas leave; however, in the event, I was to be moved again. There was very little tractor work in the dead of winter, so the last come first went. I was very sorry to leave my work-mates and my wonderful land-lady, but there were farms in the county where they were desperate for help. Going home was even more complicated this time. The Liverpool and Heysham boats were both off that night, so I had a twelve-hour train journey from Birmingham right up to Stranraer. As before, I sat on my case in the corridor, as did a lot of other people. When we reached Carlisle, luckily there was a great exodus; from then on, a sailor and I had a whole side of a carriage each to stretch out and doze on, a great luxury. At least the crossing was only a three-hour one after that.

Chapter Eight

Lowland Farm, Oxhill

IN JANUARY I WAS WRITING: 'I think I'll be all right here. They
are very good people and feed and look after me well. They work
terribly hard themselves as they are so short of labour. They have
three hundred acres and only an old man, George, a middle-aged man
named Will and a boy of sixteen also called George, who lives in the
house. There are three in the family: Mr and Mrs Shire, who are
fairly elderly, and a daughter whose name is Ann. The other daughter,
a teacher, is married. They can get no one to help in the house,
which is nice and big and well-kept but all stone-floored downstairs
and cold, even with a log fire lit in the evening in the sitting-room.
We have our meals, except supper, in the kitchen where it's warmer
in the day. They have a wireless there, so we hear the news, but
that's about all. There is no electricity or water laid on except for a
pump over the kitchen sink. We have an Aladdin lamp in each
downstairs room which gives a good light'. The outside lavatory was
a short walk away down a brick path and contained an Elsan.

'We have breakfast between 6.45 and 7, and slither out in the
snow at 7.30. Mrs Shire mixes a big bucket of gruel for the calves
and does it up with milk in other buckets and we cart it round to
them. First of all I go down to the barn and, by the light of a hurricane
lantern, fill a sheet (split sack) with hay and take it round to three
lots of calves in different directions, four sheets full. By that time
their hot drinks are ready and I take them round. There are three
little calves with curly white foreheads, as the bull is a Hereford. In
the next pen of five there is one rather thin little one that has to
have the bucket held up for her to drink out of. One of them butts
the bucket about the floor and is a nuisance. Then there are four

Mrs Shire and Ann.

that have meal and chaff to follow their hay, then eight that have hay alone – it's like a hotel! Twenty altogether. Then they all have to be cleaned out. Mrs Shire and I attack this.' (Later I did them on my own.)

'Then I take old Percy the bull out to the pond for a drink, following Mrs Shire's instructions: you open his door a bit, push a wisp of hay at him, catch the ring in his nose and clip the bull-stick on to it, then open the door and lead him out. He is very quiet but I don't take chances. We plod down to the water, at which he whoofs for a while; sometimes I get fed up waiting and push his nose under a bit. At last he starts drinking and if I lean against his side I can hear the water gurgling down his throat and going splash into his stomach; he must drink gallons. Then I take him back and shut him in again. What a boring life! We unloose the cows after milking and clean out the stalls.

'If it's not too windy, we fill and start the tractor, George and I, and Mr Shire takes him off to drill slag, a sinister, black, extremely heavy substance raked out from under furnaces in iron or steel works, that contains phosphates. It is done up in small bags of one and a

Percy's morning drink.

quarter hundredweight and these are emptied into a thing like a seed drill, a long box on wheels with shaking-out apparatus. You hitch it on behind a tractor and it distributes the stuff evenly over the field in a strip nine or ten feet wide. Slag-drilling is a filthy job, so young George does it; the dirt doesn't worry him, and he can manage the weight of the bags. I go with Will and the horse and cart and help with whatever he's doing. We come back about 4.45 and I help to feed calves, empty the tractor radiator and do any other odd job till 5.30.' When Mr Shire saw how busy I kept, I said I had to, as it was overtime. At this he was very disgruntled and said it was their ordinary hours, so rather than feel I was robbing him I ended up doing it for nothing, as I couldn't go in while they were all busy outside.

'When the other horses have been unharnessed, I go down to the field to catch Paddy (so named because he was bought from an Irishman), who works in the mornings and has to be at hand. They think he must have been ill-treated by a man, for he'll not come near one. He's a lovely big horse, as good as gold so far. He must approve of me, for though he sometimes rambles round a bit and pretends he's not coming, he then stands patiently while I put the halter on him and then we fairly trot over the ridges and furrows to the gate. All three horses are very good-natured.

'The snag is that I'll be working every second week-end, as George and I take them alternately. However, I have a longer week-end once a month, from Friday evening, which gives me time to get away.

'*26th January*, 1945. Oh, I do wish it would thaw. I have chilblains all over my feet, though they aren't too bad if I wear two thick pairs of socks and my gumboots. I also have them all over my knees again. Mrs Shire has lent me some ointment; I must get some more calcium. Even in this fierce cold I can keep warm most of the day wearing an extra jersey under my overall, but not my overcoat, as it's too heavy to work in except on the tractor. We have not been able to do much ploughing. Old George and I have been loading and carting manure. As he is not too good on his feet, I deal with the horse and cart, help to load, lead and tip it, and he pulls the stuff off at the back with a special fork. Beauty is the old mare's name; she is a very good worker, backing and turning well. We also go down for a load of hay,

Part Two *Lowland Farm, Oxhill*

which George hacks out of the rick with a heavy hay-knife, rather like cutting cake. Dear, the feeding all these animals take when the snow's on the ground and they can't find anything for themselves.

'Tysoe is a village twenty minutes' walk away and Oxhill is about fifteen minutes in the other direction. A film comes to the village hall on Tuesdays, but I don't feel like turning out these nights; I get so chilly when I've come in and sat about a bit. Now I'm beside a lovely big log fire. I wish I could sleep down here!

'*1st February*. Thank you very much for the parcel. I've been lathering Velvene Balm on my hands; even the palms were chapped. At last it's thawing and the last two nights I've been really warm and not woken up half chilly.'

I used to put on a spare pair of big socks and a jersey over my pyjamas, put my overcoat over the bedclothes, do a lot of exercises, jump into bed and try to get warm. Though I had a big stone very hot jar, the parts of the bed that it didn't touch were icy. Any drop of water spilt near the wash-stand froze solid almost at once, and I was apt to skate in my room. One night I left my bakelite mug half full of water and in the morning it was nearly solid. Even in a comfortable room before a blazing fire my back still shivered, with two jerseys on and slacks.

'The kitchen isn't like ours, warmed by a range. There's just an open fire low down with two little ovens at one side. It cooks very well but doesn't throw out much heat. When I think how I used to rejoice in snow and frost! I still would if I could do some tobogganing and skating. The oddest thing of all was watching drops stop and freeze before my eyes as they ran down the tractor radiator while I was filling it.

'Oh, I did rejoice in the thaw, hearing a great dripping all round the yard. My first job that morning was to shovel away the night's thick snow to make a path round. The mildness of the last few days was lovely, and to be able to change into a skirt and silk stockings in the evening without feeling a bit cold is such a treat. All the fowl were rushing about, able to scratch again, and the ducks and geese seemed to be bathing and splashing all the time to get rid of a fortnight's dirt.

Peaceful Wartime

'Today was springlike enough to have showers, which are still quite a novelty. Old George and I brought in three loads of mangels and then moved forty-five sheep a long way to a new field. There really should be a good dog. It seems odd not to have one on a farm; there is only a sheep-dog of sorts that chases everything and is a perfect nuisance. I'll be glad when the cows and calves can live out and there won't be such a lot of feeding and cleaning to be done morning and evening. The new calf is very frisky and rushes about when we're trying to do the pen, kicking up her heels and squawking like a doll with the squeak gone wrong – a most comical creature.

'Last night I spent till 9.15 scraping and salting two hare-skins and I hope I've cured them. Mrs Phillips used to tell me how she did them, but I'd never seen it done and my goodness, it is a rotten job getting the slimy, skinny stuff off the leathery part. When I'd finished I thought I'd have to go into the house bent double, but got back to the perpendicular with an effort. 'Every picture tells a story'. The hares made two lovely dinners. I've helped to eat three, shot by various people. The land here is covered with them.'

The hare skins didn't cure properly, after all that work. Mrs Shire had to throw them away when I was away one week-end.

'*9th March*. I have done quite a lot of setting-out fields and ploughing, and so has young George. The War Ag has ploughed one big field with a good slope to it, so there will be plenty of harrowing to do as the land gets drier. It's a very heavy, greasy soil here when it's wet, and like concrete when it's dry; a tractor gets stuck or suffers from attacks of wheel-spin very easily in bad weather.

'The new calf, whom I named Sally, is a great little thing and gollups up her third of a bucketful night and morning with tremendous verve. She is red and white in patches, with a little curl round where each horn will grow, and her great idea, if Nan is cleaning out her little pen, is to escape and frolic about the yard; it's a job to get her in again. There was a lamb born yesterday when we brought the sheep up to a field near the house. Mr Shire did the job, and the sheep immediately bunked off and left the poor limp little thing. He had a job to catch her and pen them both, but they were all right.

'Mr Shire is a fussy, worrying kind of man. He walks round the farm quite often juttering away as if everything was bound to be going wrong, and yet he is an intelligent person who has a devoted family and knows that we others are sensible enough and doing our best. It gets on your nerves sometimes; you can be working away in the barn topping mangels and putting them through the grinder for feed exactly as he said it should be done, yet you can hear him coming grumbling along and he'll utter some sort of grouch as soon as he sees you. Old George sometimes says 'Ah, whatever you do is wrong, and if you don't do nothin', that's wrong too!' Machinery worries him; he has never even learnt to drive the car or do anything to it. He admits that young George and I can handle the tractor all right, and I feel I know at least some things he doesn't, but I'd rather work when he's not there giving me the jitters too. It was quite funny the other day, when I offered to take home a big load of hay in the cart, as he wanted to stay and keep an eye on George ploughing. He said it would be much better, if I could manage it, and asked most doubtfully if I thought I could. I said yes, of course I could, as I've been taking up all the loads of hay with old George; I've been wagoner for him since I came, to save his feet. It's awkward getting through some of the gates that have a bad approach, but Beauty, the cart and I used to shoot through some very narrow gateways when the place was in such a slush with snow that you nearly had to swim through or founder.

'I was backing the empty cart into the hovel one day when Mr Shire came and shouted at the mare because I touched the post with the cart. I wish these men wouldn't shout at the animals; it only bothers them and makes them awkward. Though I said I'd done it all right several times before, he told me not to. Next day there was no one there to put the cart away, so I did it, asking Mrs Shire, who was there, not to say anything. She is quite different and much better to do anything for. Ann is so quick and brisk that she makes me feel slow, but I'm sometimes more thorough, as I notice on a Monday morning when I've been away and she's done out the calf-pens. She's a very nice girl, though, aged about thirty. We get on well and have a good laugh when we have time. She is small and pretty, with blue eyes. She's a member of the Young Farmers' Club, which has films and lectures. I went with her to a meeting last week and am going to a social with her tomorrow evening.

'Recruiting for the Land Army has almost stopped, I believe. They should make it a bit more inviting and give some encouragement to those who want to go on with farming or have small-holdings of their own after the war, instead of making such a difference between us and all the other military and civilian services. I never expected a tip when the war ended, but I see no more reason why Civil Defence should get one than the W.L.A., or why ex-land girls don't need any help to set up in business or training for something else if the A.T.S. do. Some of the Civil Defence had an awful time during the bombing, but so did all the hospital staffs, and I haven't seen anything about nurses getting a bonus!

'I was digging the garden one or two days last week for what old George calls 'beayuns'. I wished it had been our own; however, I'm glad you've got someone to do it. On Sunday I felt energetic before dinner and mowed the lawn for Nan with a rather blunt mower. The leather bootlaces you sent are much appreciated by the family here and by me. They find it impossible to get anything that will last, leather being unobtainable.

'Thank you, Dad, for the chocolate and this writing pad, and both of you for your letters. I got the parcel just as I was going out with the tractor, and took a bit of chocolate with my lunch basket. It was a most beautiful day, clear as could be, and I was rolling and harrowing a wheat-field higher up than the farm-house, whence I had a good view all round. The land is flattish for some distance round here, but Edgehill of the battle rises quite high in a long ridge a couple of miles away behind Tysoe. The harrowing was to pull up the squitch and 'tiller out' the roots of the wheat to thicken it, which sounds a bit contradictory.

'Did I tell you I have also been harrowing wheat with Jane, one of the mares? I did three fields and rather enjoyed it, though I needed an extra pair of socks to pad my boots with. I heard – from Mrs Shire! – that Mr S. said he'd never had the job done better. Jane is a very good worker; she sets off at a great pace in the morning, once I have her 'geared up'. For a few days she was what they call 'collar-proud' because she hadn't been working for some time and didn't want her collar put on. The collar weighs quite a bit, hames and all, as you stand beside her in her box coaxing her to put her head into it; the saddle's heavy too but just goes straight on, and the rest is routine tightening of buckles. As the afternoon wears on she tends to get a bit awkward each time she comes to the end of the row nearest home. She turns very neatly at the end of the row; I hardly have to guide her, as she seems to feel where the harrows have to go.

'I like brushing down the horses if ever I have both time and energy; I hate to see them with days'-old mud and loose hairs on them. Jane has a beautiful chestnut coat. She obviously enjoys grooming and stands still except when I get to a ticklish spot just above her hind fetlocks. Aren't you supposed to be particular about their legs? Anyway I don't stand just behind them.

'Yesterday morning just before breakfast there was great shouting and calling of 'Paddy!' from Mr Shire and young George and eventually an agitated face appeared at the window to call Ann. She dashed off and had him in a minute. George had tried to drive him in without even taking a halter; as I couldn't forbear remarking, 'It's no good: he's an Irishman and won't be druv!' One of us could catch him easily but the men could run about the field all day after him.

'Yesterday was market day in Stratford, and they took in four fat cattle and a cow and calf. The calf was a beautiful one, just two days old and fetched £7:5s! Mr Shire bought two little calves, red-and-white, and a very large black pig for Ann which is to farrow early in April. She has weird ears that flop right over her face. The other black sow and family are getting on famously. Everyone stops to look at the little pigs. She produced them with no fuss, rather unexpectedly; I was in cleaning her pen before I noticed all the other inhabitants, and she wasn't at all cross when I admired them. Her name is Caroline, and she follows us all round the yard like a dog as if she likes company.

'I think Churchill might have reckoned up the number of Irishmen in the forces, not to mention the thousands of men and girls in munitions (earning good money, I grant you) and on the land and in hospitals over here before he started making lamentations over 'the exception'. It's like these parsons who say 'as many as are here present' in a gloomy voice with a condemnatory look at the congregation.

'Are Johnny Malcolmson's harrows those big drags that need two horses? I suppose so. I just had three small harrows. That field beyond Mrs Carey's – I shouldn't like to get too near the edge with a tractor; it keeps falling away. I'm sure it looks well now, though.

'Yes, I've been wishing the blessed calves could go out by day, but it's a job to find somewhere to put them that won't mean walking a long way to drive them in at night. Eight of the biggest are to go into a field where there are sheds for them at night. We've had the same lovely weather as you for weeks. The hawthorn is full of buds and the blackthorn is nearly over. My face is about its summer colour and my arms are getting quite brown. Just fancy your seeing a wooden plough! I wish you could get a photo of it for me.'

My cousin Mélanie, who had been in the WRNS, had married in India and come home to have a baby. 'I've heard from Aunt Mary that the baby is to be christened Mélanie Claire and called Claire.' I saw her, aged three weeks, a contented little soul with a quiff of fair hair sticking up all along the top of her head.

'*18th April*. The crops are all safely in, bar a couple of acres of mangels and potatoes. We drilled the barley a fortnight ago. George has been rolling wheat and I spent most of today rolling eight acres that I horse-harrowed. We put big wooden road-bands round the tractor-wheels between the spade-lugs so that they don't do much damage. Do the chain-harrows at home not have spikes? Because ours have, I thought they all had. They chain-harrowed a clover field and gave me the job of walking up and down picking up all the big stones I could see; I didn't think much of that. However, most of the clover is well-grown and you can't see a damn!

'It's been so hot lately that work has been a burden, and we never seem to finish before six o'clock. We go out after tea and a bit of bread and butter about seven, or just after the headlines of the news, and work till 9.30, when we spend nearly half an hour having breakfast. Dinner is a movable feast, usually at one. I think the idea is to have half an hour, but it usually spins out a bit. I'm not in any hurry anyway, as I'm entitled to an hour, especially as I do half an hour a day extra for nowt. I often think I wouldn't mind going back on the War Ag in some tractor depot and get away from it at knocking-off time or get my overtime without feeling I'm taking his last penny.

'I do the odd half-hour's digging in the garden in the evening, as they are very behind-hand. An airman, Ron Lawson, has taken to cycling over quite often and is very energetic, not having any exercise on duty. He is a decent chap and has helped a lot. He says the war in Europe will be over before this moon's finished, so I hope he's right'.

When he first came, with some other airmen, I was asked to cut some slices of ham, but was mildly admonished for making the helpings too big; I was a bit surprised as I'd seen the huge pig cut up and salted down. Ron told us about his decoration – 'That's my line-shoot' – but I'd have admired him more if he hadn't, somehow.

Mr Shire continued to nag on every occasion or none, and finally I got exasperated one morning and gave him my notice over the radiator of the tractor; it was nearly a dead heat! After that, till I went, he was as nice as pie; I was really quite amused. Mrs Shire was always nice, and we wrote to each other occasionally.

While working in Oxfordshire for a while in 1947, I was asked over to the Shires' and went on the early 'workmen's bus' a number of times on Tuesday, my day off. I enjoyed setting-out and ploughing a couple of fields for fun, doing some harrowing and climbing up to pick the last of the apples off the tops of the trees. Mr Shire steadied a forty-foot ladder for the highest one, saying 'My, you have got a reach!' After a good lunch and tea, they sent me off laden with fruit.

Chapter Nine

Hill Farm, Shipston on Stour

HERE AGAIN, they were said to be in desperate need of help, this time with milking; however, it was done by machine. Here again, as at the Shires', I succeeded a gem of land girls. I had heard so much at the last farm about Mary, who had left to be married, and all she had done, that I didn't feel much joy in hearing how wonderful Phyllis was. She was there to see me in, as it were, and was very nice. I wonder if Mr Shire sang Mary's praises to herself while she was being such a paragon? It would be nice to think so, but I doubt it.

'Phyllis does the fowl, and general work between times. I've heard her say there's been many a time when she's been too tired to eat. I

Hill Farm, Shipston-on-Stour.

Mrs Watson and Graham.

know that feeling too. They take it for granted that you're as strong as a man when you're doing a man's job. Funny, ain't it? I do rather object to 'mauling my insides out' just to be taken for granted, though I hate to be inferior to someone my own size.

'I have not learnt to milk. I can put the machines on the cows – nearly all the cows, I should say – and remove them. Then I carry two steel two-gallon buckets with lids down to the dairy, heave each one up to the top of the cooler and tip the milk in gradually till it has all run down a thing the opposite of a radiator, with cold water running through the inside, into a big churn underneath. I change the churn for another when it's full, bowl the full churn to the side, make out the label for each and save the milk for the school and milk and cream for the house. Graham strips the last few drops from the cows each morning after the machine's been taken off. He is down getting the cows in by seven o'clock and I go down at 7.30 when there's some milk nearly ready to go down.

'The herd is pure-bred Ayrshire with beautiful up-curving horns. Unfortunately the breed is noted for spitefulness, I believe. They scrawb each other with their horns and leave scars, and when a newly-calved cow goes back among the herd, the others run at her and ill-treat her horribly unless she is put back with them gradually, under supervision.

'*19th June, 1945*. Last Wednesday, Graham was otherwise occupied, so 'the old chap' (Mr Watson) drove the cows in and we proceeded to do the milking on our own. He did the odd jobs, washing the udders and so on, and I put the machines on and off. All went well till I went back to pick up one bucket and its machine from where it stood between two cows, and one of them lashed out at me 'without I touched her' and gave me a horrible bruise from mid-calf to mid-thigh, which is now turning pretty colours. I seized the nearest stout broom and whacked her good and hard (getting as bad as the men, but they tend to whack if the cows are even restless) but she had another try or two, looking frightened, so in the end Mr Watson got the bucket away. Oddly enough, she had been milked without any trouble. We went on all right then till we came to an old tartar that kicked me a bit while I was putting on the machine, grazing my arm.

Graham milking with Alfa-Laval machines.

Then, as Mr Watson would try, in spite of my entreaties, she kicked him in the cheek and nearly knocked him out. We left her for Graham to deal with when he turned up at last. We finished at 6.45 instead of 6; what an afternoon! However, it's not likely to happen again. I never did fancy that job much, though helping is a different matter. Milking breaks the day up well and makes the time go faster.

'That nasty cow had another go at me this morning when I took the machine off, but I was standing too near for her to do more than wipe her mucky hoof on my overall. I'm not going to have any more to do with her; it makes me too jumpy. Incidentally, it's nonsense to say, as I've heard said, that cows never kick straight backwards: that's exactly what she did. Graham wasn't a bit impressed till I rolled up my dungarees a few days later and showed him the bruise about a foot long.

'The family consists of Mr and Mrs Watson and three sons. Ted, the eldest, is forty and doesn't do much beyond fetching the German prisoners for work in the morning and taking them back to camp at night. The other two, Graham and Derek are quite a lot younger and do most of the work.

Graham with part of the pedigree Ayrshire herd.

'Derek has cut two fields of hay (Sat. and Mon.) and we hope to be haymaking by Wednesday if it keeps fine and warm. No, the position is still the same for land girls, victory in Europe or not: it's still our busiest time, so there's no chance of leave in the summer. They have even quite a lot of thrashing to do, but the Germans will do that, thank goodness. We've singled and hoed the mangels and they look fine, and we're now hoeing kale in the same field. There was one rather steep field where I was horse-hoeing. One of the Germans held the hoe and I led Captain, a seventeen-hand grey horse. Each time we turned at the top of the field, I was dangling on the bridle, trying to keep out from under his huge feet while he crossed them over to turn; it was a bit hair-raising.

'*26th June.* The last few days the weather has been so wet that we've had to 'pack up' the haymaking temporarily. We've been planting sprouts, at least the Germans have, after I've clipped the roots and placed them on the rows. George, the Italian, went back to camp today, so I suppose I'll have the cowsheds to clean. We've also been sprinkling sulphate of ammonia round the sprouts from a large bucket that you lug along the rows. I've had an energetic day keeping ahead of the Germans, except Gustav, who works at the same pace. I hear ten striking, so must go down and have some supper and go to bed. Glad you were able to make some goosegog jam. Mrs Watson has been making a lot of blackcurrant jam and some red-currant and strawberry and amber gooseberry. I spent a couple of evenings helping her to clean the fruit, so as to be able to eat the jam with a clear conscience.

'Sure, I'll put my cross for the old man (Churchill) but they think the Labour man with get in for here. It's Rugby division.'

Haymaking was very hectic. There was a lot of clover in the hay, and it was picked up while still very green and heavy. When it came up on the elevator it flopped on to the rick in great wreathed-up wodges that nearly knocked me over. I wrestled with it as hard as I could, forking it over to Gustav who was strong and heavily-built, a farmer himself. When I could no longer shift the latest mass, he murmured 'Leave it,' stuck his pitchfork in, and seemed to heave half the rick over to his side: a wonderful sight, and I blessed him. He must have been in his forties, imperturbable, with a lean, craggy face. His mate Albrecht was a smaller, pink-faced, cheerful man who was a pig-farmer at home. I only once met a Nazi type, stiff-necked and inclined to lecture, so we left him to it and called him Adolf.

'Well, fancy having a car again – how exciting! I hope she runs well, and long life to her. I suppose she's almost new, having done only 1700 miles?

'We had that thunderstorm on Saturday week too. It was really spectacular – lightning all round for miles but no rain for ages. We finished haymaking nearly a fortnight ago and are now baling one of the six ricks; at least Ted and three prisoners are, while the other is thatching a rick nearby. I am making the pieces of thatch, yelming the straw first; that is, straightening it by putting a bundle on the ground and running my hands from the middle to each end of the straw till my nails get worn down.

'We spent all last week thrashing the last six corn ricks (at this time of year!) up at Greenhill, the other part of the farm some distance away. I used to cycle up after the milking and breakfast, taking sandwiches and drink in a haversack. It was fairly cool and there was a bit of a breeze most of the time, so it wasn't bad. I was on the rick. The drum, a pretty new one, is fitted with long pipes down which the chaff and cavings are blown wherever you want them; thus no one has to cart the rubbish or stand in it and get smothered. We had the elevator placed at the back to take all the loose straw up to the straw rick, where one man could deal with it. We had only six people on the job. At the Abbey we usually had ten, but two were raking out the rubbish all the time, one was pitching straw and there were two or three on the straw rick; also there had to be someone to feed the drum, but this one has a small canvas on which the corn can be dropped and which feeds it evenly down inside. All the same, I think we got on a bit faster there than here, and we trussed the straw, which makes it far handier to use.

'Sorry this is so uninteresting, but I'm writing in a hurry after wasting half the evening pottering about to see if they wanted to shut up all the various lots of ducklings and goslings. They, i.e. Graham, Mr Watson and Derek, left it till dark to round up one lot of ducks and had a fearful job chasing them up from the brook. By the time that's done and we've had supper, it's bedtime. Mrs Watson gets fed up and says she'd rather do the job herself, only it's very difficult for one person. They always pop off when it's time to do them and say 'Leave them,' and then it gets dark.' We were always having to collect the creatures into their pens in shelter when it rained; it seemed funny for water-birds to be so delicate, but they were. To complicate matters, when it rained, Graham had to run and get a cap or he would end up with a headache.'

Before haymaking for about five weeks I had spent most of the day between milkings in singling and hoeing roots, often by myself for hours. It got harder on the back, not easier, as time went on. Graham used to come and join me in hoeing at times and talk about the farm and the family. He had had a twin brother who had died at birth, and I often thought he somehow missed him. He and Derek had been company for each other till Derek began courting a girl and was always 'scortin' off' to her place in the car, to Graham's disgruntlement; nothing would persuade him that this was to be expected. On Sunday afternoons Eric and the girl would lie peacefully side by side on the horsehair sofa in the kitchen, which was also a passageway from the back kitchen to the rest of the house. It was really the dining-room and had a handsome chiffonier, as Mrs Watson called it, with a big looking-glass above it. Mrs Watson cooked excellent meals. She had a girl who came in to help in the house on week-days, and Graham and I washed up on Sundays. The dish I specially remember was jugged hare which we had a couple of times during harvest. I was almost too tired to be hungry by half-past eight or nine, but it certainly revived my appetite. Graham used to say I ate more than he did, and sit admiring the way I put away platefuls. All the same, he was pretty substantial. He was quite tall and had nice features and curly brown hair. We had such rich milk from the Ayrshires that we always took a lot of cream from the churns, knowing that they would be left with more than the three per cent of butter-fat required by law.

The house was a handsome three-storey one of Cotswold stone, three windows wide, with the top windows set in little gables, nearly dormers. There was a beautiful spiral staircase of bare polished oak twisting up the back of the house, with an unusually tall window to light it. My room was at the top in front with a pleasant view of the lane, bordered by trees on the left, running down to the village. The snag was that I had to carry water up the two flights, wash in a basin from head to foot every night and cart down the dirty water in a slop-bucket in the morning without spilling a drop on the stairs. The earth-closet lavatory was even further from the house this time; to reach it you went across the yard and right down the vegetable garden.

On Sunday afternoons, if I was not on a home weekend, Mrs Watson took to asking me into her bedroom where she sat and rested, to talk to her and maybe knit or mend. She was stout and pale, with dark eyes and dark hair piled up on her head. She had high blood-pressure and sometimes when busy downstairs and irritated, would go off like a rocket at whoever was near her; that was rather upsetting, but generally she was good-natured. Derek, on the other hand, was usually critical and sarcastic, and it was not often that his sharp features relaxed. Ted was big and red-faced with fuzzy fairish hair. Nobody took any notice of 'the old chap' as Mr Watson was called.

Part Two *Hill Farm, Shipston on Stour*

They said he had gambled away family money long ago. The two younger brothers didn't think much of Ted, who did so much less work than either of them and just shouted at them if they grumbled about it.

One evening when I came across to the house after washing and scalding the equipment in the dairy, Mr Watson was at the back door and an unholy row was coming from the inner kitchen. I went and looked in at the three men rampaging round the big solid dining-table, roaring like a herd of bulls at each other, and wondered what on earth was going on. It was like a scene from *Cold Comfort Farm*; as long as they didn't come to blows it was really very funny. 'Wait here and let them get on with it', said Mr Watson, so we leant against the back doorposts till the noise died down, or rather the 'creating and doing-about', to use Graham's favourite expression.

Occasionally Graham would suggest going to the pictures at Chipping Norton and drive me over. One night on the way back we went to walk round and look at the Rollright Stones, a big prehistoric circle on the hillside, with another smaller group; they were supposed to be impossible to count. I had seen them by day, but they looked even stranger in the slightly hazy moonlight.

Sometimes I went to Mrs Wilkinson's for the week-end from Lowland, or Hill Farm. Other times I went up to Birmingham, but it was too far to cycle there. I remember at least once plodding along a busless road in uniform, trying to get a lift from cars that just swished past. One evening I was invited to watch Graham shooting rabbits, and got landed with carrying a couple home. I wouldn't have touched them if I'd known they were crawling with fleas, which I brushed off my arm from time to time; luckily that was as far as they got. There were dozens of rabbits killed when we cut corn; I was allowed to take one to my aunt and uncle, but was charged three and sixpence for it! Aunt Mary made a delicious dinner of it; Uncle Jack said she made it taste like chicken. One evening he came rushing downstairs shouting 'There's a mouse in my room!' in such mock-terror, for a burly man, that he had us in fits of laughter; when my aunt recovered, she went up and set the trap, and that was that.

Harvesting went fairly well. Of course Derek did the tractoring and

Peaceful Wartime

I was just a human-operated pitchfork, with Graham grousing that I picked up only one wheat-sheaf at a time to his two. I retorted that I wasn't his size, and preferred to place each sheaf conveniently for the person loading the trailer; that didn't convince him any more than when I tried to get him to sharpen my hedge-slasher later on. He always put me off and I was left hacking with a blunt weapon. He was a funny mixture. Once, after great preamble, he asked me if my teeth were real. He thought they were too good to be true, I don't know why, as the bottom ones are rather uneven.

Victory in Europe Day was rather flat. Everyone dispersed in different directions, though there was a bonfire on the hill for the villagers. Eventually Graham came in and we walked up to it and then went for a quiet pint in the local.

'Well, we finished harvesting last week, amid hindrances of rain as usual, except for a bit to be thrashed load by load near here. That wouldn't take half a day if it would keep fine but it's pouring tonight. Fancy your having eight glorious weeks! I've rubbed that well in here. The English climate is really appalling – beats the Irish one for cussedness every time.

'Of course we're thatching ricks now all the time. Two of the Germans are doing it, and it's a most monotonous job for me, yelming straw all day, not hard, but it makes your shoulders ache. I have a kind of wart on the sole of my foot, which hasn't stopped me from working fourteen hours a day on it – oh no, we did actually sit down to meals, so subtract two hours.

'What sort of jobs are there at the B.B.C.? When I enquired, they only wanted typists.

'Yes, they want land girls, and they'll give them damn-all when they've finished with them. I never expected a gratuity or clothing grant, but we seem to be the only service getting nothing and, after all, there are only 50,000 of us. Only recently did I read that the W.L.A. heads had argued our case urgently several times, only to be turned down flat by a grudging Churchill. The uniform they're allowing us to keep is too funny for words. One wonders what we're supposed to wear between the shirt and the shoes! They may alter that, though. I don't want my coat dyed navy.'

Warrenpoint and Carlingford Lough

A Car Again!
My parents in the "nearly-new" Morgan 4-4, 1945

Peaceful Wartime

In the event, we did keep it all and it was most useful for gardening. I kept my good brown overcoat, but it was only three-quarter length.

Graham and I finished the thatching at Greenhill and took photos of each other up on the rick. When I was alone there each dinner-time I used to read *Horizon* or *The Poetry Review* with my sandwiches, sitting on a pile of old straw. One day I looked up, caught a movement across the rickyard and watched fascinated while a stoat did a weird kind of playful dance, advancing, rolling over down a big heap of rubbish and repeating the sinuous pattern over and over for about fifteen minutes. There was no other animal in sight; it didn't seem to be stalking, but kept up this concentrated ritual until it was out of sight. No one I have told seems to know what it meant.

Harvest Thanksgiving in church that year was a great occasion. I really enjoyed standing in line with the three farmers and their parents, singing 'We plough the fields and scatter' at the top of our voices. I think of the Watsons every year when we sing it. Graham and I wrote to each other occasionally during the next two or three years, so I heard about Derek's broken engagement and the state he was in for a good while, dashing about in the car half the night; and about the tremendous increase in farm machinery at Hill Farm, with which Derek did a lot of contract work. Some of that I saw on a later visit with my cousin Dudley.

My parents had bought a new house and were due to move at the end of October, so I applied for my discharge from the Land Army on the 10th. Mrs Watson seemed surprised and rather put out at this, but now that the worst of the war was over, I had no wish to stay on. I was looking forward to getting home, sorting my possessions for the move and helping my parents. Indeed I could not have borne to miss all the excitement.

Considering his initial disapproval of my going farming, I was glad my father managed to comment on my two and a half years: 'You stuck it well.'